TEACHING SCOTTISH LITERATURE: CURRICULUM AND CLASSROOM APPLICATIONS

To Jim
with love &
best wishes,

Alan

1/6/98.

SCOTTISH LANGUAGE AND LITERATURE
General Editor
Douglas Gifford
University of Glasgow

Assistant Editor and Project Convenor
Dr Beth Dickson
University of Glasgow

Advisory Team
James N. Alison
Her Majesty's Inspectorate (rtd)
Dr John Corbett
University of Glasgow
Anne Donovan
Hillhead High School
David Drever
Kirkwall Grammar School
Morna Fleming
Beath High School
Gordon Gibson
University of Paisley: Craigie Campus
John Hodgart
Garnock Academy
Alan MacGillivray
University of Strathclyde
Dr James McGonigal
St Andrews College, Bearsden
Jan Mathieson
Ardrossan Academy
Dr Elaine Petrie
Falkirk College of Technology
Ronald Renton
St Aloysius' College
George Sutherland
Scottish Qualifications Authority

Other volumes in the series:
Scottish Literature: A Study Guide
Edited by Douglas Gifford and Beth Dickson
Language and Scottish Literature
John Corbett

Thanks are due to Professor R. J. Lyall whose vision and hard work developed the postgraduate courses from which this project grew. Thanks are also due to Jackie Jones and the staff of Edinburgh University Press who were consistently encouraging and saw the proposal through to publication.

Teaching Scottish Literature: Curriculum and Classroom Applications

SCOTTISH LANGUAGE AND LITERATURE, VOLUME 3

Edited by
ALAN MacGILLIVRAY

EDINBURGH UNIVERSITY PRESS

Edinburgh University Press
22 George Square, Edinburgh EH8 9LF

Typeset in Linotype Jansen
by Koinonia Ltd, Bury
and printed and bound in Great Britain

A CIP record for this book is available from
the British Library

ISBN 0 7486 0930 X

'... I marvell gretlie, I yow assure,
Considderand the people and the ground,
That ryches suld nocht in this Realme redound.'

(Sir David Lyndsay, *The Dreme*, ll. 838–840)

CONTENTS

EDITOR'S FOREWORD

When Sir David Lyndsay of the Mount is taken by Dame Remembrance on a conducted dream tour of the Universe (in his first long poem, *The Dreme*), he is shown the damned souls and corrupt clergy in Hell, the planetary gods in their spheres, the blessed denizens of Heaven and the many regions of the Earth. After he inspects the earthly paradise of Eden, Lyndsay's thoughts naturally turn to his own country of Scotland and he begs Dame Remembrance to show him it in detail. He sees all Scotland's riches in natural and human resources and is impelled to ask why it remains so poor, gaining no benefit from all its apparent wealth.

Disregarding (but not forgetting) Dame Remembrance's explanation of how Scotland remains poor and unfulfilled because it lacks good government, there is a metaphor to be extracted from this for our purposes in this volume (and its companions in the series). We hope that one of the things that readers will realise, or be reminded of by their own Dame Remembrance, is that Scotland is a rich nation in its literary culture. Just as Lyndsay sees the wealth of Scotland in terms of its natural resources of food in the plant and animal life on land and the fish in its seas, its extensive mineral deposits and the positive qualities of its people, so readers should be able to see the cultural wealth of their community in terms of the linguistic resources of three languages – Gaelic, Scots and English – expressed orally and in literature, the sophisticated variety of a literature that has always had a European dimension and been part of the great cultural movement of our civilisation, and the strength of an individuality created by the specific qualities of Scotland and its people.

Why therefore, we might ask with Sir David Lyndsay, should these riches not redound within this realm, or be displayed to the advantage both of themselves and of the community they adorn? This volume will address the question of why Scottish literature has not been and is not being given the attention in Scottish schools that it so much deserves;

yet it will not linger on old unhappy things like social, educational and personal discrimination against the traditional culture and languages of Scotland. The more important purposes of the volume are to put all that discredited and indefensible prejudice firmly in the bin of history where it belongs, to show that the riches of Scottish literature are there for the enjoyment and profit of all students and teachers in our schools and colleges, and to encourage teachers by means of a wide variety of exemplars to bring Scottish literature and language topics into the forefront of their planning and teaching concerns.

The exemplars provided here are not, as teachers will see, cast in a form suitable for immediate application to an SCE class requiring practice in examination technique. Such a format would be both space-consuming and insulting to the professional expertise of our readers, who are well able to take out of these exemplars the basic ideas and suggestions and develop them in the ways most suitable to their classes and departmental policies. Besides, the format of the external examinations is currently under review and it would have been foolhardy to tie exemplars to examination requirements that might change while the book is at the press or within a year or two of its publication. We feel that it is not the function of such a volume as this to be examination-led. We have the more ambitious long-term purpose of influencing the future nature of assessment of language and literature in Scottish schools as part of a major change brought about in the courses that lie behind the assessment.

After choosing the epigraph from Sir David Lyndsay and writing the opening of this Foreword, I discovered (or, rather, Dame Remembrance reminded me) that the quotation had been used for an identical purpose by the editors of the famous report produced in 1976 by the old Scottish Central Committee on English, *Scottish Literature in the Secondary School*. I feel that this is in fact a happy coincidence and I have retained the quotation for this volume. Two of the present contributors, James Alison and Douglas Gifford, were members of the subcommittee behind that landmark in the promotion of Scottish literature in Scottish schools, so that there is a physical link between that report and this volume. In a very real sense, everything that has been published on the subject during the last twenty years has been inspired by that familiar blue-covered document, and nothing that it said so eloquently then has been superseded or rendered irrelevant. Let this volume stand as a tribute to the work of the individuals behind the report, so many of whom are sadly no longer among us.

I am grateful to Professor Douglas Gifford for the invitation to edit this volume and bring within its compass a goodly number of the issues and ideas that many of us have been trying to promote and develop over the last quarter of a century. My thanks go to many people who have been instrumental in making this volume possible. First of all, there are the individual contributors who have managed to write so eloquently and authoritatively on their different subjects while coping with the pressures and multifarious demands of their daily teaching and administration. Then I have to thank a number of people for specific help in a variety of ways: Dr Beth Dickson of the University of Glasgow Scottish Literature Department for the administrative arrangements that made the management of the contributors' working group possible; Morna Fleming, Beth Dickson, Anne Donovan and Gordon Gibson for developed exemplar materials; Jackie Jones, Nicola Carr and the staff of Edinburgh University Press for their interest and patience throughout the lengthy process of preparing the volume. Finally, on a more personal level, I have to thank my friends and co-workers on the Association for Scottish Literary Studies Schools Committee for their companionship over many years; their enthusiasm and commitment in so many discussions and joint ventures have been the necessary underpinning of this structure.

Alan MacGillivray

Part I Scottish Literature

1

·————

SCOTTISH LITERATURE AND THE CHALLENGE OF THEORY

Douglas Gifford and Neil McMillan

In the confusing diversity of new approaches, terminologies and catchphrases, from poststructuralism and deconstruction to 'Death of the Author' and 'Desire of the Mother', to the further confusing differences within what seem at first to be single movements such as the debates between French and American approaches within Feminist theory, the teacher and student of Scottish literature – let alone English and American – might well be forgiven for simply not wanting to know. With such plurality of views, and such frequency of what seem like fashionable changes of opinion, why should the new theories be regarded as a proper challenge? How can they help students read texts like *The Justified Sinner*, *Sunset Song* or *Mary Queen of Scots Got Her Head Chopped Off*?

We will argue that a general awareness of – if not agreement with – the major new ways of approaching literature and language studies can enhance both teacher and pupil awareness of texts, and in particular Scottish texts. Those teachers who have undertaken to teach works such as *Sunset Song*, *The Cone-gatherers* or *Consider the Lilies* already realise that issues of power, class and linguistic dominance have to be confronted, revealing a multiplicity of perspectives on Scotland and Britain, and often too a multiplicity of personas behind which the author is often concealed. The critic of Scottish literature has often had to be an *ur*-deconstructionist and the most recent and postmodern work in prose, poetry and drama has heightened the challenge to the point where it cannot be ignored. Moreover, Media Studies in Revised Higher already accepts that challenge; its Examination Board guidance incorporates much of the new theory, while in the same document Literature clearly operates within an older ideology.

To attempt to explain current literary theories in such a short space – especially when so many of these theories centre on the difficulty of lucid, efficacious and objective explanation – is a well-nigh impossible task. What we propose to do, therefore, and at the risk of brutally simplifying a highly complex field of study, is to provide points of entry into each of the main theoretical debates, in a language as accessible – as 'jargon-free' – as possible. Bearing in mind that there is no theory without practice, we will attempt in each case to provide brief examples of possible readings of Scottish texts, thus keeping the connection between the literature and the theory alive, and to suggest a range of texts which seem particularly amenable to consideration from new theoretical perspectives. And finally, we will indicate where recent debates are suggesting that there may be ways of reconciling old and new ways of reading.

There is no generally accepted canon of literary theory; that said, there are various anthologies which contain many of the seminal theoretical texts, and which provide useful introductions to – as well as suggested further reading for – the various fields covered here. One such volume is *Modern Literary Theory: A Reader*, edited by Philip Rice and Patricia Waugh. Catherine Belsey's *Critical Practice* provides a lucid and accessible guide to modern theory, and is particularly useful in the readings of texts it uses to demonstrate the theories it describes.

References and further reading

Belsey, C., *Critical Practice* (London: Routledge, 1980).
Rice, P. and Waugh, P. (eds), *Modern Literary Theory: A Reader*, 3rd edn (London: Arnold, 1996).

THE ORIGINS OF CONTEMPORARY THEORY: AGAINST HUMANISM

In Scotland, the present practice of teaching literature in secondary schools – and within certain university literature departments resistant to change – is based on the values of the dominant mode of thought extant in the West, that of liberal humanism. Broadly speaking, since the Renaissance, Western thought has sought to place man, closely aligned with God (man as the son of God), at the centre of the universe, as unique and autonomous maker of meaning, civilisation, order and progress. One of the most enduring expressions of this is to be found in Descartes' 'I think, therefore I am', a statement which posits 'I' unproblematically as the subject of 'think', and, further, as the ground of being itself. During the nineteenth century, however – and as an effect perhaps of the acceleration of capitalism, and correlated disorder and suspicion – thinkers like Marx, Freud and Nietzsche began to question and displace man's centrality, suggesting that uncontrollable factors such as the economy or the unconscious determine us more than liberal humanism accepted, and that we are thus denied the universal perspective of the superman, since there are structures which precede us in which our 'identities' are constructed, and which we must learn to analyse and manipulate.

The current orthodoxy of the teaching of literature (as opposed to media) in schools has, however, remained unmoved by such tremors. Pupils are still taught to read works primarily to identify their meaning, a meaning intended by an author who is still regarded as the guarantor of that meaning, and who is still the central figure in the literary sphere of humanism. This meaning may indeed express doubts or contain ideas of a Marxist or a Freudian nature, but it is always resolved into a stability which can be extracted from the work and verified as true (by consulting authorial biography, for example). This author is never thought of as anything other than the master of his own discourse, showing us the truth about ourselves through the media of poetry, drama or fiction – all of which are regarded as windows on the world, or reflections of how things are. And while in the end it may be justifiable – indeed, necessary – to hold to a version of such a view, it is surely desirable that teachers of literature should have considered the challenges of new theory to it, and why they choose to accept or reject these challenges.

LANGUAGE AND DIFFERENCE

If twentieth-century literary theory can be regarded as building upon the spirit of suspicion at the heart of Marxist, Freudian and Nietzschean thinking, its most significant extension is the transference of such suspicions into the field of language. While doubts about language as a medium by which autonomous individuals name and describe external reality have existed since Plato, it is only since the Swiss linguist Ferdinand de Saussure's *Course in General Linguistics* (1915) that a coherent account of language along these lines has been in place. By shifting the focus of study from a diachronic base (studying a subject over time – the traditional method of linguistic enquiry) to a synchronic one (where the subject is regarded as arrested in time), Saussure was able to show that no language translates into another in any simple, direct fashion. For example, while we have two different words for a sheep and its meat (mutton), the French use just one (*mouton*). The relationship between signifier – the written or spoken form of a word – and signified – the concept or referent – is never natural or absolute, but rather arbitrary and dependent on conventional social agreement which differs from culture to culture and language to language. In other words, there is nothing about a sheep which suggests our name, or any other language's name, for it. Therefore the sign 'sheep' cannot have any meaning in isolation – it has meaning (or 'value' in Saussure's terminology) only in its negative differentiation from other signifiers. A sheep is a sheep because of what it is not within the sign system – in this instance it is not cooked, not ready to eat and therefore not mutton – and it is this difference which is the condition of possibility for meaning.

What these considerations suggest is that language can be seen as a system which precedes us, and in which we are constituted as soon as we begin to speak or write. As Emile Benveniste has noted, it is not possible to say 'I' meaningfully without its difference from 'non-I' ('you' or 'her'), which suggests that we should no longer regard the individual human as he or she who conditions and controls a sign system, but rather as a subject of that system, and meaningless outside it. Language can perhaps never come to a close, never rest on a final signified, for that signified is always another signifier. In a dictionary, a word can only be defined by reference to more words.

References and further reading

Benveniste, E., *Problems in General Linguistics* (Miami, FL: University of Miami Press, 1971).
Saussure, F. de, *Course in General Linguistics*, trans. W. Baskin (London: Fontana, 1974).

STRUCTURALISM

Such linguistic theorising does not suggest that external reality, or the individual, do not exist, but rather that they have no meaning outside of a sign system. The kind of theory to which this gave rise began to analyse works of literature in terms of intrinsic rather than extrinsic meaning, attempting to understand a text by the way in which its constituent parts relate to one another. In the school known as Russian formalism, theorists like Vladimir Propp took traditional folk tales and broke them down into a number of building blocks common to each story. In America, *New Criticism* examined poems as if they were absolute objects frozen in time, their meanings only generated by the relations between the words within them. And in France, these practices developed into the theory known as structuralism. This theory works on the principle that narrative has a grammar whose general rules apply to the makeup of every story. In other words, each narrative has the structure of a basic sentence, with a subject, predicate and object or complement. The work of Roland Barthes was pivotal in these developments. His 'Introduction to the Structural Analysis of Narratives' in *Image, Music, Text* demonstrates the principles of structuralism with reference to James Bond stories, while he applied his theories in non-literary fields such as fashion, reminding us that written and spoken languages are not the only kinds of sign system open to analysis. (Barthes is engaged in semiology – the study of signs in general rather than just language.)

Structuralism is now largely outmoded, at least in the mathematically applied form of its hey-day in the 1960s. But structuralism broke with tradition in that it ceased to regard the literary work as an organic entity and began to understand it as a system; it is where this project breaks down that the most complicated, yet arguably the most interesting, manifestations of theory emerge.

References and further reading

Barthes, R. 'Introduction to the Structural Analysis of Narrative', in *Image, Music, Text*, trans. S. Heath (London: Fontana, 1977).
Greimas, A. J., *Semantique Structurale* (Paris: Larousse, 1996).

See also the essays under the headings 'Russian Formalism' and 'Structuralism' in Rice, P. and Waugh, P. (eds), *Modern Literary Theory: A Reader*, 3rd edn (London: Arnold, 1996).

IDEOLOGY AND SUBJECTIVITY

It is where structuralism and later Marxist thought intersect that highly important theoretical issues concerning identity emerge. Louis Althusser's 'Ideology and Ideological State Apparatuses' (1971) indicated a radical division within Marxist thought in that it no longer regarded the economic base – the unity of productive forces and relations of production – as the absolute determining influence on the 'superstructure', which comprises law and the state, as well as religious, ethical and political ideologies. While for Marx ideology, determined by the economic base, was 'the system of ideas and representations which dominate the mind of a man or a social group', Althusser's conception of a superstructure which enjoys relative autonomy from that base gives rise to a different formulation. Throughout the superstructure's ideological state apparatuses – religion, education, the family, the legal system, politics, trade unions and culture – Althusser claims that ideology works in the '"representation" of the imaginary relationship of individuals to their real conditions of existence'; in other words, that ideology interpellates or 'hails' (the figure suggesting being accosted by a friend on the street) individuals as 'free' subjects, masking their real relation to the forces of production which define them. Rather than being a conceptual process whereby one class dominates another, ideology, in Althusser's definition, operates at all levels, in a multiplicity of forms, and enjoys a certain invisibility as it is the way we think of ourselves as 'really' living.

The most important suggestion in all this for literary theory is the idea that saying 'I' may not constitute a statement of free subjectivity, but rather indicates misrecognition and participation in a structure prior to us. Ideology cannot operate without discourse, and each discourse – or domain of language use – chains us to it even as it tells us we are free. Thus 'subject' has a double meaning – one is both subject of and subject to ideology. Fundamentally, however, ideology is contradictory, and this is what allows us to pierce its invisibility, see beyond what we regard as our 'natural' being and understand our construction in it. To exemplify in a Scottish context, while the ideology of liberal humanism tells us we are each free autonomous individual human beings, the ideology of Calvinism and its work ethic can also define us in relation to work and subject us to its hierarchies and its different values.

The theories of Etienne Balibar and Pierre Macherey develop such views of literature as ideological form in greater detail, and describe how we are taught to read – particularly with regard to the standard forms of classic realism (the still predominant form in popular literature, film, theatre and television drama) which operates around the concealment and revelation of an enigma) – in order to identify with characters, and/or with the author, in a process which allows us to discover the 'truth' about ourselves. Literature is a particularly effective form of ideology because its fictive production of effects of the real ('real*ism*') resolve ideological contradictions irresolvable in real life. It is in a text's silences, argues Macherey – what it cannot account for or resolve – that ideology is exposed for what it is, and these gaps are where any effective analysis must begin.

Certain literary works not so bound to the form of classic realism, however, refuse this 'smoothing over' process, and consciously draw attention to the structures of ideology their characters inhabit. One such work in a Scottish context is Janice Galloway's *The Trick Is To Keep Breathing* (1987). The novel's fragmentary narrative form works to foreground Joy Stone's dispersal across the various subject positions or roles offered to her by ideology, none of which can contain her or offer her stability. The discourse of women's magazines, of the nuclear family, of the medical profession and of Calvinism are just some of the contradictory ideologies at work in producing her subjectivity and in precipitating her breakdown. In highlighting these positions as fictions rather than natural states of being, the novel demonstrates the state-reinforcing and imaginary factors at work as in Althusser's description of ideology, thus showing the fictive, constructed nature of meaningful existence itself.

References and further reading

Althusser, L. 'Ideology and Ideological state Apparatuses', in *Lenin and Philosophy and Other Essays*, trans. B. Brewster (London: New Left Books, 1971).

Balibar, E. and Macherey, P., 'Literature as an Ideological Form', *Oxford Literary Review*, Vol. 3, No. 1, 1978; sections reprinted in Rice, P. and Waugh, P. (eds), *Modern Literary Theory: A Reader*, 3rd edn (London: Arnold, 1996).

Macherey, P., *A Theory of Literary Production*, trans. G. Wall (London: Routledge & Kegan Paul, 1978)

POSTSTRUCTURALISM/DECONSTRUCTION

Roland Barthes' *S/Z* marks a pivotal point in the history of theory in that it both signals the limits of structuralism and hints at something beyond. Attempting to reduce the Balzac short story *Sarrasine* to a combination of codes typical of classic realism, Barthes argues that the language of structuralism he employs cannot fully contain the literary object which it is supposed to describe. This failure of metalanguage – a special language designed to describe the conditions of discourse while itself escaping these conditions – points up structuralism's own failure as a pure science, and suggests that there are no absolute boundaries between critical discourse and the literature that discourse is supposed to read internally. This also foregrounds the main problem with Althusser, who believed that he could develop a scientific, 'subjectless' discourse which could structurally account for ideology while itself escaping its interpellations and constructions. With *S/Z*, and with Jacques Derrida's critique of structuralism in 'Structure, Sign and Play in the Discourse of the Human Sciences', the borderline between intrinsic and extrinsic, so essential to structuralist thinking, is perceived as having dissolved, and the relationship between reader, text and author seen as much more fluid.

As Barthes straddles that divide between structuralism and poststructuralism – later named as 'deconstruction' by Derrida – the conception of the literary object moves from work to text, as is described in the seminal article by Barthes (with the same title: 'From Work to Text', in *Image, Music, Text*). The work – the idea of which is to some extent still central to structuralism – is delimited by a physical space (it is a book on a shelf); it can be assigned to a genre (tragedy, romance, epic and the like); it can be directly interpreted for its meaning, which is stable across time; it has an author who can be appealed to as guarantor of that meaning; and it affords a certain satisfaction as the reader consumes that meaning. The text, however, is the work opened out in a methodological field. No longer are the boundaries of the book nor the limits of genre recognised, for the text does not close on a final signified (recall here the discussion of Saussure); rather, the unlimited play of signification connects other works to the one being studied in an operation described as 'intertextuality'. The author's intentions no longer count, for his 'I' in the text, according to Barthes, is no more than a paper-'I' and no more immune from the movement of language than any other sign. Thus the reader no longer interprets, consumes and stands off, but rather participates in the production of the text, becomes part of its play in a signifying practice which unites reading and writing. The pleasure of the text is an open-ended pleasure, theoretically infinite, since to come to rest on a final meaning would be to deny discourse its proper flow.

Such pronouncements, of course, do not pass unchallenged, in particular Barthes' dramatic declaration of the death of the author. The author, of course, is not dead; and were the text to be exposed in its absolute infinite play it would be truly unreadable, beyond even the apparently endless circulations and digressions of a novel as difficult as Joyce's *Finnegan's Wake*. It is altogether a question of degree, and deconstruction – particularly that practised by Derrida – often proceeds from a rigorous analysis of those borderlines which threaten to constrict reading, paradoxically drawing and breaking lines as it proceeds. Derrida – ostensibly a philosopher, but deeply concerned with philosophy as imbedded in language – recognises that the author's meaning is present in the text, but never absolutely; following Freud and Jacques Lacan, he posits that language has an unconscious and hidden structure already in place, which the conscious mind of the writer can never fully control. Derrida's own texts, elliptical, playful and forever questioning, always attempt to draw attention to their own blind-spots, hesitating before conclusion as they deconstruct essentialist ideas of a *logos*, or God-given meaning, to which we can appeal as a central authority.

Deconstruction, therefore, is not something that is done to a text, for all analysis takes place within the textual frame set up, often utilising the very discourse it hopes to untangle. Derrida's famous pronouncement from *Of Grammatology* – 'Il n'y a pas de hors-texte' ('there is no outside-the-text') – recognises that the text exists wherever there are referents, and does not halt at the literary or philosophical work. The text extends everywhere there is discourse, and thus anything is subject to the dislocations of deconstruction (Derrida has written on topics as disparate as Plato, apartheid, drugs, nationalism, human and animal rights, love, the media and AIDS). His work is always guided by a profound respect for difference and otherness, always rigorously suspicious of the 'is' of identity.

Amid these complications, it may now be helpful to sketch out a possible deconstructive reading of a Scottish text. Hugh MacDiarmid's *A Drunk Man Looks at the Thistle* has spent much of its critical life being moulded into some sort of coherent structure and meaning by writers. MacDiarmid's biographer, Alan Bold, typically focuses on the poem's statement 'The thistle rises and forever will!' as its final signified. Closer readings of the poem, however, show that the symbol of the thistle is always disintegrating into something it is not – moon, silken leddy, octopus, the drunk man's soul – in a transformational play which refuses to rest on any one meaning. Indeed, the poem serves as a useful paradigm for the failure of the humanist quest for the *logos*, for final meaning; for the drunk man himself is forever attempting to work out the puzzle of man's soul generally and Scotland in particular without achieving satisfaction. The thistle is forever rising but also spending itself, the phallic imagery here pointing not only towards a sexual significance, but to the defeat of a single, total way of understanding the world – the defeat of metanarrative, and the metanarrative perhaps of liberal humanism itself. In the end, the drunk man's only resolution is to 'tak it to avizandum' – in other words, to defer judgement indefinitely. While traditional criticism may focus upon this negatively, a deconstructive reading would affirm such deferral as the proper and unresolved state of meaning itself. The truth is not to be found in fixed forms, but in the shape-shifting of the thistle – or the sea-serpent which writhes with irreconcilable contradictions throughout the poem. The poem thus becomes – in line with its movements of intertextuality – not only part of the text of Scottish literature, but also, in an anachronistic play, part of the fabric of poststructuralism, the reader joining the drunk man in the text in a constant doubling back over the problematics of its signs.

References and further reading

Barthes, R., 'The Death of the Author', in *Image, Music, Text*, trans. S. Heath (London: Fontana, 1977).

Barthes, R., *S/Z*, trans. R. Miller (London: Jonathon Cape, 1975).

Barthes, R., 'From Work to Text', in *Image, Music, Text*, trans. S. Heath (London: Fontana, 1977).

Derrida, J., *Acts of Literature*, ed. D. Attridge (London: Routledge, 1992).

Derrida, J., *Of Grammatology*, trans. G. C. Spivak (Baltimore, MD and London: Johns Hopkins University Press, 1976).

Derrida, J., 'Structure, Sign and Play in the Discourse of the Human Sciences', in *Writing and Difference*, trans. A. Bass (London: Routledge, 1978).

READER RESPONSE THEORY

The way in which poststructuralist thought privileges the place of the reader in the interpretation of texts has similarities with another branch of theory which is, however, based on quite different premises: that of reader response. The German branch of this approach, sometimes known as the aesthetics of reception, proceeds from phenomenology rather than linguistics in attempting to isolate the way in which (in the terminology of Wolfgang Iser) a reader concreticises a text – in other words, brings it into meaningful existence by participating with it in a reading. H. R. Jauss maps out the difference between the 'horizons of expectation' we bring to a work and the way that work confirms or transgresses those horizons as 'aesthetic distance'. American versions of this thought focus upon psychology, for example, and the way in which what Stanley Fish has termed 'interpretive communities' determine what a text means more than the text itself.

This approach clearly offers a bewildering number of perspectives for Scottish readers (urban readers of Mackay Brown? Catholic or Protestant readers of *The Sash*? Women readers of *The Big Man*?). It's useful to consider the work of James Kelman (and some of his controversial followers) in the light of differing reader response to his work. On the one hand valued for the integrity, authenticity and humour of content and style, and on the other lambasted for corrupting language and for dealing with subjects alien to the tradition of the novel, the reception of Kelman and his school demonstrates the way in which the expectations of different interpretive communities are confirmed or subverted, and how these different receptions produce varying ideas as to what this work actually 'means'. Considering how many different readings of Kelman's fiction different interpretive communities might come up with could usefully demonstrate the innumerable reader responses a text can generate. As with the other theories outlined here, it becomes very difficult to stipulate any 'true' meaning of a work with such an approach, and as with these other theories, recognition of the relativity of reading is precisely the aim.

References and further reading

Fish, S., *Is There a Text in This Class?* (Cambridge, MA: Harvard University Press, 1975).

Iser, W., *The Act of Reading: A Theory of Aesthetic Response* (Baltimore, MD and London: Johns Hopkins University Press, 1978).

Iser, W., 'The Reading Process', in R. Cohen (ed.), *New Directions in Literary History* (London: Routledge & Kegan Paul, 1974).

Jauss, H. R., 'Literary History as a Challenge to Literary Theory', *New Literary History*, Vol. 2, 1970; sections reprinted in Rice, P. and Waugh, P. (eds), *Modern Literary Theory: A Reader*, 3rd edn (London: Arnold, 1996).

ANGLO-AMERICAN AND FRENCH FEMINISM; GENDER STUDIES

One huge area undoubtedly marginalised by the liberal humanist tradition's conception of itself is that of women. Feminist literary theory – hand in hand with its counterparts in the sociopolitical fields – has done much in the past thirty or so years to change that. There is, however, a significant split within feminist theory – between Anglo-American and French feminisms – which provides an important perception of the confrontation between traditional approaches to literature and more recent poststructuralist dislocations. Anglo-American feminist theory, very broadly speaking, begins with the task of seeking out the specifically female literary tradition which has been suppressed by male-dominated literary institutions. This move for equal rights within the canon – typified by Elaine Showalter's 'The Female Tradition' – seeks to uncover women's texts and identify continuities between them, keeping them and their tradition distinct from the established male tradition. Applied to Scottish literature, this would mean that to focus solely on male writers in establishing a separate tradition would be merely to repeat the mistakes of the overly centralised English canon by excluding the women's tradition. It can be seen that the paradigm offered to explain Scottish Renaissance literature – obsession with the lost Eden of the golden age and a lost mythology, insistence on the return to racial roots, to older language, overt nationalism and socialism – applies mainly to male-authored texts (Gunn, Gibbon, MacDiarmid, Linklater, McColla, Muir). Women's writing of the period – that of Catherine Carswell, Willa Muir or Nan Shepherd – often has a radically different emphasis, focusing, for example, on immediate domestic restriction rather than timeless spiritual communion with the land, and satirising present claustrophobic convention rather than evoking an ideal past, or emphasising a need to escape rather than asserting a will to build Scotland anew. This approach challenges received and male-managed theories concerning the period, emphasising the value of women's experience to be found in literary work and opening out the male-dominated canon. It is striking to observe how recent republication of texts by Scottish women has revealed a women's tradition and brought into existence a new market for the circulation of hitherto largely ignored women's writing.

There are other avenues within this theory. Class and race enter as claimants, with the call to recognise both a working class and a black women's tradition (women of colour are often already marginalised by male writers of their own race, as well as by white institutions). Lesbian critics have suggested that literary institutions are not just sexist but heterosexist, and have pointed to a different body of women's experience within a lesbian literary canon. The poet Jackie Kay – female, Scottish, black and lesbian – is a significant case in point for

Scottish literature here; her work often emphasises the validity of her experience of occupying several marginalised subject positions simultaneously.

The problem with Anglo-American feminist theory, from the French perspective, is that while it works to uncover a plurality of women's experience distinct from that of men, and in so doing provides a challenge to the male orthodoxy, it is in this very insistence on experience and consequent sidelining of questions of language that such an approach begins to repeat the mistakes of the very institution it is trying to subvert. In other words, Anglo-American feminist theory operates within that traditional approach to literature which views the text as transparent, as a window on the world framed by the vision of the author whose presence is sought as a guarantee of meaning. If this humanist tradition is undeniably a patriarchal one – 'man' is at the centre of the humanist ideology in a far more gender-specific sense than 'humankind' – then to substitute woman for man at its centre is not to subvert, but merely to reproduce the existing order, without analysing its perception of itself as the absolute and natural status quo – which must necessarily exclude all that it cannot account for in order to survive.

French feminism expresses itself in a heterogeneous group of theories which owe more to the broad church of poststructuralism than the kind of traditional criticism favoured by the Anglo-American school. French feminism's three prime movers – Luce Irigaray, Julia Kristeva and Hélène Cixous – are all markedly different in approach, but can be loosely grouped together around their reinterpretation of the ideas of the psychoanalyst Jacques Lacan. Lacan posits that when the child first begins to speak and learns to differentiate 'I' from 'non-I', he or she effectively enters the symbolic order, a realm governed by the Name of the Father – the central authoritative figure in the Oedipal triangle – which conditions the success of all logical, masterly communication. Simultaneous with this, however, is the creation of the unconscious, which enters into the gap between the 'I' which speaks and the 'I' which is spoken in the utterance. The unconscious is the province of the Desire of the Mother, and works to disrupt the phallic, linear logic of the symbolic order. Language becomes feminine in its gaps, its silences and ellipses, as well as the points where rhythm and sound overtake the direct communication of stable meaning.

This is controversial and complex theory, heightened in difficulty by the refusal of its proponents to present logical and coherent arguments in support of it. Rather than succumb to the tyranny of the symbolic order, its texts often proceed by indirection and allusion, as if demonstrating *l'écriture feminine* (what Cixous terms feminine writing) by binding theory and practice into one. It is important to state, however, that such discourse is as likely to be found in male-authored as female-authored texts; it is not biological but symbolic gender that is at stake here, although notions of 'writing the body' veer close to a conception of the essential, eternal feminine. What is valorised is transformation as a weapon against totalitarianism; to view language as an ever-shifting series of perspectives (what Kristeva calls the subject-in-process) is to transform our fundamental way of looking at the world.

French feminism is closely aligned with deconstruction, and it is not difficult to adapt the reading of *A Drunk Man Looks at the Thistle* to its main criteria. The phallus in this poem is under attack from many sources, not least of which is the 'silken leddy' – a shadowy and protean female presence which comes into existence at the limits of the protagonist's attempt at logical discourse and does much to undermine it. In a similar way, the many female figures of fantasy projected by Jock McLeish in Alasdair Gray's *1982 Janine* prove larger than his attempts to master and control them, predicating his collapse into a heterogeneous textual collage of voices in Chapter Eleven. The subversive power of such literary play is perhaps most acutely felt, in a Scottish context, in Janice Galloway's *Foreign Parts*; here, Cassie's invigorating, constantly transforming discourse disrupts and discredits the monolithic, myopic language both of the tour guides and of the snapshots of Chris, Cassie's remembered lover.

Even were the Anglo-American and French feminist approaches able to be reduced easily to coherent and opposing schools of thought this would in no way signal the end of feminist literary theory. As Annette Kolodny has remarked, feminist theory is by and large 'a playful pluralism, responsive to the possibilities of multiple critical schools and theories, but captive of none'. Beyond questions of the canon and of *l'écriture feminine*, feminist approaches to literature incorporate the kind of Althusserian ideological-materialist analysis described above, exemplified by the work of Catherine Belsey in *Critical Practice*, as well as attending to more general areas of subjectivity as constructed in class, race, gender and sexuality. This area – more generally known as 'gender studies' as it is as much concerned with notions of masculinity as with femininity – has made its presence felt within Scottish literature with the publication of *Gendering the Nation*, a collection of essays which offers lucid and detailed readings of Scottish texts within this framework .

References and further reading

Belsey, C., *Critical Practice* (London: Routledge, 1980).

Belsey, C. and Moore, J. (eds), *The Feminist Reader* (London, Macmillan, 1989).

Cixous, H., *The Newly Born Woman*, trans. B. Wing (Manchester: Manchester University Press, 1986).

Eagleton, M. (ed.), *Feminist Literary Criticism* (London: Longman, 1991).

Gifford, D. and Macmillan, D. (eds), *The History of Scottish Women's Writing* (Edinburgh: Edinburgh University Press, 1977).

Irigaray, L., *The Irigaray Reader*, ed. M. Whitford (Oxford: Basil Blackwell, 1981).

Kolodny, A., 'Dancing Through the Minefield: Some Observations on the Theory, Practice and Politics of a Feminist Literary Criticism', in E. Showalter (ed.), *The New Feminist Criticism* (London: Virago, 1986).

Kristeva, J., *Desire in Language: A Semiotic Approach to Literature and Art* (New York: Columbia University Press, 1980).

Lacan, J., *Ecrits*, trans. A. Sheridan (London: Tavistock, 1977).

Moi, T., *Sexual/Textual Politics* (London: Methuen, 1985).

Showalter, E., 'The Female Tradition', in *A Literature of Their Own* (Princeton, NJ: Princeton University Press, 1977: reprinted London: Virago, 1978).

Showalter, E., *The New Feminist Criticism* (London: Virago, 1986).

Showalter, E., 'Towards a Feminist Poetics', sections reprinted in Rice, P. and Waugh, P. (eds), *Modern Literary Theory: A Reader*, 3rd edn (London: Arnold, 1996).

Whyte, C. (ed.), *Gendering the Nation: Studies in Modern Scottish Literature* (Edinburgh: Edinburgh University Press, 1995).

POSTMODERNISM

Postmodernism is perhaps the most vigorously debated term in contemporary cultural theory and has as many definitions as there are thinkers on the subject. In terms of literary history, it names the period beginning roughly with the end of the Second World War and continuing today – that is, the period following modernism. It identifies those literary works which are conscious of themselves as fiction; which privilege the image over the referent, or the signifier over the signified; which refuse to settle on a single, authoritative point of view; which play games with genre, style, narrative and history; which ask of the reader a practical collaboration in the production of meaning, often 'including' him or her as a character in the text along with the author, as in Gray's *Lanark*; and which generally affirm the sense of disintegrating values and communities prevalent in the twentieth century, rather than bemoaning their loss, as modernist works are prone to do. Postmodernism is less of a theory than a practice; writers like Alasdair Gray, Emma Tennant, Sian Hayton, Frank Kuppner and to some extent the Alexander Trocchi of *Cain's Book* and the Irvine Welsh of *Marabou Stork Nightmares* are some of the major Scottish exponents.

The term postmodernism, however, is not peculiar to literature and in no way ends in naming a literary genre; it was in fact taken from the discourse of architecture. It is best understood not as an '-ism' but as postmodernity, the set of cultural conditions under which we now live, dominated by consumerism and mass media: we are less defined by who we are and where we come from, and more constructed in terms of the clothes, music, cars, homes, food, newspapers and television programmes we daily consume or use. Within postmodernity stable identity dissolves (the so-called 'dissolution of the subject') within the differential systems of cultural relations, and to this extent the discourses of poststructuralism, ideology and French feminism, described above, are all inextricably bound up with the postmodern and have their part to play in describing it. More positively, if we are aware of our postmodern condition, we can see how we are constructed, see that which is 'other' or alien to us, and see that that which is different and exists at the margins is as valid as that which we previously thought was central. Indeed, through this perception the margins come to occupy a more powerful position, since the centre is reduced to being a mere strand in the heterogeneity of the contemporary cultural fabric. The implications for writing and reading contemporary Scottish literature are obvious; the Scottish writer/reader no longer needs to operate with subservience within cultural hierarchies, and no longer need assume inferiority in subject matter or language. The astonishing burgeoning of recent Scottish writing is evidence that the Scottish writer is today indeed aware of her or his postmodern condition. Within this condition (analogous to Derrida's text to which there is no outside) rigid hierarchical binarisms – male/female, white/black, straight/gay, high culture/low culture and so on – dissolve. To analyse contemporary Scotland in terms of postmodernity is to acknowledge a plurality of cultural differences, each as valid as the other. This is the position towards which current critical thought in Scotland is now shifting, as for example reflected in journals such as *Cencrastus*, *New Edinburgh Review* and, most recently, *Scotlands*.

References and further reading

Brooker, P. (ed.), *Modernism/Postmodernism* (London and New York: Longman, 1992).

Docherty, T. (ed.), *Postmodernism: A Reader* (New York and London: Harvester Wheatsheaf, 1993).

Jameson, F., *Postmodernism, or the Cultural Logic of Late Capitalism* (London: Verso, 1991).

Lyotard, J.-F., *The Postmodern Condition: A Report on Knowledge*, trans. G. Bennington and B. Massumi (Manchester: Manchester University Press, 1984).

POSTCOLONIALISM

If our postmodern condition teaches us a healthy respect for the other – that which differs from us – then postcolonial theory opens out this question to examine the cultural production of those nations once defined by the Western powers which occupied them. Writers like Edward Said subject the imperialism of Western thought to a rigorous critique, examining, for example, how the West's sense of itself was often defined against its own conception of an Oriental, underground self. A controversial instance of a postcolonial attack on white critical orthodoxy is Chinua Achebe's assault on Joseph Conrad's *Heart of Darkness* (1902), a text which Achebe finds to hold up the dominant Western image of Africa to the extent that it 'teems with Africans whose humanity is admitted in theory but totally undermined by the mindlessness of its context and the pretty explicit animal imagery surrounding it' (Achebe, 1980). Conversely, and providing a stimulating comparison, Stevenson's *The Beach of Falesa* (1891) is a surprisingly early attempt to expose the arrogance of Western and British imperial attitudes towards native cultures.

The application of postcolonial theory to Scottish literature is now under way. In a paper published in *Scotlands*, Berthold Schoene argues provocatively that 'many Welsh, Irish and Scottish people perceive themselves as citizens of colonised nations which neither represent fully equal constituents of Great Britain nor independent member states of the Commonwealth', a situation which calls for the analysis of Scottish writing in terms of its relation to dominant English culture. Scottish complicity in the English/British imperialist project being put aside, Schoene's reading leads him to making controversial statements about Scottish literary history – which, according to the postcolonial paradigm, proceeded through identification with the imperial power in the time of the makars, a 'nostalgic phase' in which Scotland produced no writing of any consequence (the eighteenth and nineteenth centuries), and a period of myopic and mythic totalising constructions of Scottish national identity (the cultural renaissance of MacDiarmid and others). Only now is Scottish writing realising its postmodern heterogeneity, according to Schoene, a view which reduces the literature of the past to a totality against which our new-found plurality can be affirmed and valorised. His view may be unacceptable to many readers of Scottish literature in its unwillingness to allow that some of the best of writing may be based on premises with which its readers do not agree – do many readers not willingly suspend their disbelief for the pleasure of reading Milton, Hopkins, Hogg, Muir? – but it challenges us to reassess the validity of many of our underlying assumptions concerning 'Scottishness', forcing us to see the changing nature of national identities, and to question the values inherent in their transformations.

References and further reading

Achebe, C., 'Viewpoint', *Times Literary Supplement*, 1 February 1980, p. 113.

Ashcroft, W., Griffiths, G. and Tiffin, H., *The Empire Writes Back: Theory and Practice in Postcolonial Literatures* (London: Routledge, 1989).

Bhabha, H., *The Location of Culture* (London and New York: Routledge, 1994).

Said, E., *Culture and Imperialism* (London: Chatto & Windus, 1993).

Said, E., *Orientalism* (Harmondsworth: Penguin, 1985).

Schoene, B., 'Scottish Literature and the British Postcolonial Condition', *Scotlands*, Vol. 3.

NEW HISTORICISM

The criticism often made of theories such as postcolonialism, postmodernism and poststructuralism, as Schoene's argument demonstrates, is that in totalising the past together with the implicit value judgement 'bad' against present 'postmodernism' and the implicit value judgement 'good', critics avoid an understanding of history and thus ignore its many complications. The work of Michel Foucault has opened a new way of linking history and literature, by viewing history in the minutiae of its power relations and effects. By refusing to settle on a total account of the past, Foucault's work focuses on that which is excluded ·from conventional history, charting differences in representation from one period to the next.

Foucault's thought, along with Mikhail Bakhtin's view of the text as a social act open for different uses, has produced a heterogeneous theoretical school in which history and literature are reunited, albeit in a highly critical and rigorous way. Shakespeare and Elizabethan theatre are a popular field of study for critics like Stephen Greenblatt, a typical new historicist in that he tends to focus upon the kind of place assigned to theatre at the time, and the number of highly ambiguous power relations such theatre involved. In this perspective, for example, the subversiveness of Shakespeare becomes a major issue. A parallel Scottish study might examine differences in representation before and after the Reformation, or attempt to discern the kinds of ways power circulated within the Scottish court at the time of the Renaissance, and the poetry produced in it. Whatever period it regards, new historicism always refuses to regard the literary text as privileged over, or in isolation from, other kinds of document (medical records, pamphlets, statute books), and attempts to incorporate the bias of present perspective into the structure of reading.

References and further reading

Bakhtin, M., *Rabelais and his World* (Cambridge, MA: MIT Press, 1986).
Dollimore, J. and Sinfield, A. (eds), *Political Shakespeare: New Essays in Cultural Materialism* (Ithaca, NY: Cornell University Press, 1985).
Foucault, M., *The Order of Things* (London: Tavistock, 1980).
Greenblatt, S., *Renaissance Self-Fashioning: From More to Shakespeare* (Chicago: Chicago University Press, 1980).

SOME PROBLEMS OF THEORY

New historicism in general draws attention to the kind of totalising reduction to which postcolonial and postmodern thought addresses itself, and highlights a problem which cuts across all areas of contemporary theory. In this essay recent critical developments have been set against the ideology of liberal humanism, itself presented as given without critical examination. But discussion of complexity and rigorous questioning are processes at the heart of the new critical orthodoxies. Without them, theory runs the risk of becoming like the thing it places itself against, or simply dissolving into a certain political quietism, a postmodern shrug. To affirm pluralism and difference without close attention to where differences are being overlooked or moulded into sameness by the formula which states 'everything's valid = nothing's valid' is to ignore the fundamental principles by which Western thought has gradually begun to recognise and accept the challenge implicit in the dislocations which define it.

Thus postcolonial discourse carries with it a healthy scepticism regarding its own motives. The challenges to postcolonial and postmodern orthodoxies often come from cultures where the so-called dissolution of the subject is treated with disdain; as bell hooks, the African-American thinker, notes, 'should we not be suspicious of postmodern critiques of the "subject" when many subjugated people feel themselves coming to voice for the first time?' Should Scottish readers likewise question postmodern critiques when they feel that modern Scottish literature has finally begun to articulate coherent, plural and satisfying statements about Scottish identities? Whatever we decide, we should recognise that postmodern Scottish writing is as much about bringing forth new, previously ignored or unheard voices in the work of such as Jackie Kay, James Kelman, Irvine Welsh, Duncan MacLean and Christopher Whyte – to name a disparate few – as the kind of wilful textual gameplaying which it can sometimes appear.

References and further reading

hooks, b., 'Postmodern Blackness', in P. Williams and L. Chrisman (eds), *Colonial Discourse and Postcolonial Theory: A Reader* (New York and London: Harvester Wheatsheaf, 1993).
Richard, N., 'Postmodernism and Periphery', in *Postmodernism: A Reader* (Hemel Hempstead: Harvester Wheatsheaf, 1993).
West, C., 'The Postmodern Crisis of the Black Intellectuals', in L. Grossberg, C. Nelson and P. A. Treichler (eds), *Cultural Studies* (London: Routledge, 1992).

SOME PARADOXICAL CONCLUSIONS

It can be claimed that Scottish literature is a site where all these different theories converge, in so far as Scottish culture exists in a relationship of subordination with a dominant English culture. To privilege Scottish writing is to look at a long-excluded margin and to assert its value, even before theory comes into play. Indeed, the widely held belief that Scottish writing, from the medieval period onwards, habitually engages in apparently unresolvable opposites, with internally antagonistic concepts like 'Caledonian antizyzygy', 'dissociation of Scottish sensibility', 'crisis of confidence', deemed central to the Scottish tradition, suggests that Scottish culture is particularly amenable to contemporary critiques.

This is not to say, however, that Scottish literature has always been involved in postmodernity, or deconstruction, for such theories acknowledge not only the irreducible difference of an opposition but also its inadequacy, its inevitable surrender to a third and further terms. To tie binarisms like heart/head, highland/lowland, passion/reason and so on to the unicity of an organic Scottish tradition is to over-simplify and to limit the kind of liberating opening out that deconstructive reading always involves, and to sacrifice the poststructuralist empowerment of the reader to the tyranny of an au-thoritative, if different, cultural agenda. In fact, deconstruction poses a serious threat to the kind of nationalism often at the centre of Scottish literature's definitions of itself. If, on the one hand, this kind of theory privileges the marginalised and suppressed, Scottish literature comes out strongly as a challenge to the hegemony of a central English culture. However, in so far as it seeks to close itself off and refuses to acknowledge its difference with itself, – if indeed difference is the con-dition for meaning – thus seeking a new centre, some kind of absolute essence of Scotland in its literature, it simply repeats the problems of logocentrism and ceases to be transformational. If Scottish literature and culture has thrived on paradox in the past, it may well need to do so in the future!

It is against such reductions and exclusions that theory holds its greatest promise for Scottish literature and culture. Nationalism and poststructuralism are uneasy bedfellows – but it is precisely the teasing out of these difficulties which makes the poststructuralist analysis of Scottish writing such an invigorating prospect, however slow it has been in getting started. To posit that Scottish writing may indeed anticipate postmodernism or poststructuralism (or put the 'post' of these terms into question) in its apparently endless ability to 'tak it to avizandum' while simultaneously keeping in mind the exclusions its binary philosophy maintains is the kind of open-ended approach now called for. To maintain a general sense of a national culture while continually acknowledging the margins which displace this centre and move beyond the merely national is the challenge which faces Scottish studies today if it is to engage with current theoretical developments.

In the end, the teacher and student of Scottish literature and language may still feel that 'literature' is somehow devalued by so much complex philosophical analysis and sociopolitical debate. In recent work of powerful critics such as M. H. Abrams (as in his essay 'The Deconstructive Angel', which points out that deconstructionists rely on the very communicative power of language which they deny to make their argument), and especially in the attempts to make synthesis of Coleridgean and Romantic theory with the results of modern thinking, as in Colin Falck's *Myth, Truth and Literature*, it is true that there are both strong voices for traditional humanism and against what are seen as the false premises of Sausurean linguistics (artificially separating text from voice and gesture) and the *logos*-based edifice Derrida built thereon. Critics like Abrams and Falck criticise much of contemporary theory for dealing with literature in every way but as literature, and insist on recognition of aesthetic achievement as something valuable in itself, ultimately and rightly to be seen as beyond final analysis, and not to be rationalised out of existence.

Nevertheless, the great theoretical movement has left undeniably useful – perhaps crucially useful – tools for intelligent readers. In an age where the media are manipulative in myriad ways, the need to perceive prejudice, the hidden agenda, the cliché, the stereotype, the oppressive innuendo is crucial, and however mysterious 'literature' may claim to be, it too has its hidden agendas and powerful innuendos. Judicious exploitation of the theories discussed here can open our eyes; and in Scotland, with its inheritances of sectarianism, romanticised history, post-imperial assertions and guilts, gender role allocations, uncertainties of stance towards its own and English culture, and its resultant confusion of identities, there is a responsibility placed upon the teacher and student of cultural subjects to see cultural productions from as many productive viewpoints as conceivably possible.

References and further reading

Abrams, M. H., 'The Deconstructive Angel', in D. Lodge (ed.), *Modern Criticism and Theory* (London and New York: Longman, 1988).
Falck, C., *Myth, Truth and Literature* (Cambridge: Cambridge University Press, 1989; revised edition, 1994).

EXEMPLAR I

Level/stage of school

S5/6.

Duration

1/2 periods.

Topic/text(s)

'Tam O'Shanter': a feminist critique.

Purposes

> To make pupils aware of how women are both explicitly and implicitly presented in Burns's poem.

> To encourage pupils to practise the technique of the 'resisting reader' – approaching the text with a critical suspicion, alert for the ways in which a text may be reinforcing stereotypes and unacceptable assumptions about social roles and attitudes.

Teaching approaches

1. As part of a larger study of 'Tam O'Shanter', distribute and read the poem, using appropriate audio recordings for authenticity as desired.

2. Focus with pupils on the female figures in the poem: the wife Kate, the sulky sullen dame; Kirkton Jean; the landlady; Mungo's mither; the ugly old witches; young Nannie, 'Cutty-sark'; the mare Maggie. Discuss how each may be reinforcing a female stereotype: the nagging wife, the woman of ill-repute, the sympathetic 'other woman', the suicide, the grotesque crones, the sexy young bewitcher, the loyal servant. Can they be placed into two categories: those who are dull and deserving rejection or ridicule, and those who carry a kind of glamour or attraction? Is this an oversimplification of the presentation of female personages in the poem?

3. By contrast, look at the conventionally 'male' elements in the poem: the market business, the drinking and revelry, the spending of the money earned, the male friendship, the horse riding, the hunting, the Devil's presiding over the witches' dancing, the piping, the evidence of violent

crime, Tam's voyeurism and sexual excitement, the exhilaration of the chase and escape. Are there many counterbalancing 'female' elements: keeping the house, prophecy and witchcraft, providing food and drink and favours, public dancing and display, making clothes, loyally supporting a dominant male (Maggie)? Are there 'darker' female aspects suggested: the desire for vengeance on men (the witches' chase), resentment of children (the murdered bairns)? Discuss with the pupils whether they wish to accept 'Tam O'Shanter' as a simple entertainment?

4. Have pupils produce some writing on this topic. Is Burns totally aware of the picture he is presenting of women, or is he unconsciously reinforcing the current (and still existing) bracketing of women into unexamined roles within a male-dominated society? Does such a view of the poem diminish it in the eyes of readers?

EXEMPLAR 2

Level/stage of school

S5/6.

Duration

1/2 periods.

Topic/text(s)

Sunset Song by Lewis Grassic Gibbon: a Marxist critique.

Purposes

To look at the ways in which the novel exhibits both explicitly and implicitly a social conflict between a dominant controlling class and an exploited and controlled class.

To consider the stance of the writer in relation to this conflict.

Teaching approaches

1. As part of a larger study of *Sunset Song*, read the text of the novel in the way felt to be most appropriate, whether in sections during the study or completely beforehand.

2. At an appropriate time, when the reading has been completed or is well advanced, focus with the pupils on the political aspects of the novel: the explicit political references to Conservative, Liberal, Socialist and other attitudes (refer to characters like John Guthrie, Chae Strachan, Long Rob, Robert Colquohoun, the gentry, other farmers, etc.). Do the same for references to the material prosperity of characters and other elements in the novel. Discuss how the reader is expected to react to characters in the light of their politics and material prosperity.

3. Discuss with pupils where the economic and social power lies in the society depicted in the novel. How much of it resides within Kinraddie and how much is elsewhere? How is the changing prosperity and fortune of Kinraddie affected by economic and political needs of outside forces? Again, what attitude is the reader expected to adopt towards this? Pupils in groups can begin to build up a diagram or chart of the areas of economic, social and political strength or weakness in the novel.

4. How different has the picture been at different stages of history and pre-history? Has the pattern of 'civilisation' been a constant one or have the sources of power been located in other parts of society? How does Gibbon project the topic into the future? Does he foresee any change? How does the reader react to his vision?

5. Have the pupils produce some writing on this topic. Does the novel suffer from appearing to subscribe to a particular political viewpoint? Would it be more satisfactory if Gibbon did not hold strong social and political beliefs? Indeed, would the economic and social pattern of injustice be any different if Gibbon did not bring it to the readers' notice? Would it be a condoning of an unjust system if the novel focused solely on personal issues in the story?

EXEMPLAR 3

Level/stage of school

S4/5.

Duration

2 periods.

Topic/text(s)

Short story 'Feathered Choristers' by Brian McCabe: a reader-response activity.

Purposes

To read and discuss a story with a view to finding out how it can be read and understood in different ways by different readers.

Teaching approaches

1. Provide copies of the story in sections corresponding to the divisions of the story. Distribute the first section to the pupils and read it with them. Have pupils discuss the section among themselves. They should focus on things like the basic situation, the speaker and the addressee, and their feelings about what is happening. One pupil in each group might keep a note of any very divergent ideas that emerge.

2. Read the second and following sections alternating with discussion in the same way, until the story is completed. At no time either during or after the reading should the teacher contribute any opinions or judgements about what the pupils are taking from the story.

3. After the reading and discussion are complete, the class as a whole should discuss with the teacher any variations of reading that have emerged. Can any of them be regarded as 'misreadings' *in the pupils' collective opinion*? What varying readings can be regarded as 'acceptable'? It is not the teacher's business to act as any kind of authority.

4. If desired, there can be follow-up writing by pupils inspired by the situation of the story.

Products

Pupils' writings.

Group notes on the variant 'readings' of the story.

Supporting materials

None, apart from copies of the story.

Other comments

This exercise in reader-response theory can be applied to any text considered suitable and manageable by the teacher. Note that it is *not* a prediction exercise but a developing reading of the text aimed at finding out how it is received while it is being read. With a poetry text, the divisions of the text should be much shorter; in this story they are long and based on the author's own divisions solely for convenience of handling within the space of one or two periods.

EXEMPLAR 4

Level/stage of school

S4/5.

Duration

1/2 periods.

Topic/text(s)

Three short poems: 'Epitaph on an Army of Mercenaries' (A. E. Housman); 'Another Epitaph on an Army of Mercenaries' (Hugh MacDiarmid); 'A Third Epitaph on an Army of Mercenaries' (Edwin Morgan).

Purposes

To examine how one poet influences another in a particular poem, both positively in subject and form, and negatively in reaction or disagreement.

To enable pupils to discuss the differing motives for being a soldier, and the attitudes of society towards the soldier.

Teaching approaches

1. Provide pupils with a copy of Housman's poem, read it and open up discussion about the nature of the mercenary soldier as opposed to the soldier who fights for patriotic reasons. Refer to examples of mercenary forces: the French King's Scots Guard, the Pope's Swiss Guard and the Russian Cossacks in times past; the French Foreign Legion, the Gurkha regiments in the British Army, etc., in modern times. Refer to places where mercenaries have appeared in recent times: African countries, Bosnia, etc. Does Housman's view seem very romantic and idealised? His classical studies (he was a Professor of Latin) seem to be making him think of heroic Ancient Greeks and Romans. The poem was written in

the early years of this century (*Last Poems*, 1922) but does not seem to take account of the experience of the First World War.

2. Distribute copies of MacDiarmid's poem, read and discuss. How does MacDiarmid's epitaph (published 1935) differ in tone and attitude to the subject? Is it relevant that MacDiarmid (C. M. Grieve) was a medical orderly in the First World War, or that he held strong left-wing views?

3. Do the same with Morgan's poem (published in 1994). How different is it from both the earlier poems? Is it relevant that Morgan was also a medical orderly (in the Second World War), or is he more influenced by recent research into the psychology of the killer?

4. General discussion should focus on the way in which MacDiarmid and Morgan both seem to be at odds with Housman and how Morgan seems to be reacting against MacDiarmid. Is the influence of the earlier poet in each case a stimulus arousing the later poet to disagree? Can the three poems be reconciled in some way so that each may be seen as containing some truth? There might be some scope for imaginative writing to conclude the work.

2

———— • ————

CHOOSING AND USING SCOTTISH TEXTS

James N. Alison

In this chapter we shall be urging the wider, more systematic use of Scottish literature in the curriculum. It makes sense therefore to start by considering briefly what literature is, and what particular claims it has to the time and attention of young people in our schools.

By literature we mean, for the most part, texts in the imaginative genres – poetry, drama, fiction – but we also include types such as biography, travel writing, history and journalism in which there is seen to be some creative value. The texts may be written, oral or have an audiovisual dimension. For any culture and language the field extends in principle from the earliest surviving materials to all contemporary items which are not purely ephemeral. It is from this corpus that course planners, at whatever level and with whatever criteria, must make their selections.

WHY BOTHER WITH LITERATURE?

Why should we insist on teaching literature to young people at all? Arguably it represents only one function of language – one, indeed, that may seem to most of them to have little practical or vocational application. It is true that in the recent past its position has been entrenched and largely taken for granted in Scottish education. In primary and secondary schools literature has most commonly been combined with language in one subject area called 'English' or 'English language' and it has been similarly treated in the syllabuses of the SEB (Scottish Examination Board). SCOTVEC (Scottish Technical and Vocational Education Council) has, on the other hand, identified literature and communication as distinct modules of study. In the universities courses on literature and language are generally treated as separate entities.

A concomitant of Scotland's traditional curricular planning is that since the study of literature has been regarded as an essential part of English, it has enjoyed privileged status and is virtually compulsory even at the most senior school stages. It remains to be seen, however, whether the final version of the Scottish Office's Higher Still programme, which is currently in preparation, will maintain the linkage or will enable senior students to opt out of literary study, as they may already do in FE colleges. Recent debate upon these proposals has led some teachers to look again at the justifications which can be offered for this high-profile treatment of literature.

Whatever the outcomes of Higher Still, we are convinced that the study of literature should remain an integral element of the school curriculum for English at all levels, and that it is relevant to the transactional as well as the creative uses of language. Our grounds are that:

1. literature demonstrates the fullest, most precise uses of language;
2. it gives young people access to challenging vicarious experiences and promotes their imaginative, aesthetic and moral growth;
3. it encourages them to formulate and refine their critical responses in writing and in discussion with their peers;
4. it promotes the study of language in its different forms;
5. it offers stimuli and models for students' own writing;
6. it gives students knowledge of their cultural milieu and heritage;
7. it yields reflective enjoyment.

These claims can seem high-flown and are horribly vulnerable to class realities, but they remain articles of faith to which most teachers of English will subscribe.

THE CLAIMS OF SCOTTISH TEXTS

Clearly the above considerations apply with particular force to the use of Scottish texts with Scottish students in nationally devised or recommended English courses. There can, of course, be no simple guarantee that what is taught in schools will necessarily be absorbed and appreciated by students. Overzealous promotion by the system has sometimes the opposite effect from what is intended. Nevertheless, education has as one of its prime responsibilities a duty to try to sensitise enquiring minds to their cultural heritage. If educators in a small country fail to accept and discharge this function, a potent national resource may shamefully be lost for ever. Scottish poetry, drama and prose (fiction and non-fiction) constitute such a resource.

We believe that they have important advantages which should recommend them for classroom use at all stages. They can give our students unique imaginative insights into episodes and experiences which are part of our country's distinctive past, and may influence our present and future. They help us all to understand what living hereabouts has meant to the folk who have gone before us; they give shape to ideas, casts of mind and ways of saying which have haunted Scots over the centuries and which are often with us still. In practical terms some are likely to tap into the domestic and non-standard language that young children bring to school. Many will also draw upon accessible shared experiences of teachers, students and their families or illuminate local events and places. Fascinatingly they link with our music and art, and our political, social and economic history. Overall they can help us to gain a sense of our cultural identity in relation to our neighbours and other nations. But only if we know about them.

In this context the affirmation made in the influential SCCC report of 1976 is still worth emphasising:

> A feature of this world is its tendency to develop larger and larger administrative units in government and business and for popular entertainment to become more and more homogenised and prepackaged. As this tendency grows, so does the need for the individual to discover and define himself in terms of local and national (as opposed to the international or supranational) culture.[1]

By definition the aesthetic encounters that Scottish materials offer cannot possibly be supplied from any other source. Well-meaning arguments about priorities, which warn that Scottish texts do not compare in quality with the magnificent best of Shakespeare, Wordsworth or Dickens, should not be allowed to obscure this fact. We are certainly not making the blinkered suggestion that English courses in Scotland should ignore worthwhile texts from the cognate literatures of the English language, including those of America, Ireland, India and the Caribbean. We do, however, assert the principle that at all stages, whenever practical choices come to be made, course design should start from a central core of carefully selected Scottish recommendations, and should move out from there as generously as possible.

WHAT COUNTS AS SCOTTISH LITERATURE?

Mischievously echoing T. S. Eliot, a recent essayist has asked, 'Is there a Scottish Literature?'[2] Pronouncements on the teaching of Scottish literature have mostly dodged this awkward question and avoided defining their subject area – presumably on the assumption that we all know what we are talking about, don't we? This evasiveness may after all prove to be a wise strategy since any attempt to map the ground is likely to stir up vexatious boundary disputes. However, for the purposes of planning school courses it seems worthwhile to try at least to identify some of the landmarks of our terrain.

The following criteria ignore the vexed question of what constitutes 'literary quality' and do not therefore serve to identify a canon of Scottish masterpieces which are authoritative in our culture; they also avoid arcane speculations about 'antisyzygy' and the 'reductive idiom'. They are merely markers of a putative Scottishness in texts, a mixture of features of language, subject matter and the experiences and backgrounds of authors. The fact that they are hybrid does not mean that we should be apologetic or defensive in deploying them to identify a working corpus of Scottish literature. If a piece meets any one of these requirements, we should be happy to label it 'Scottish': many will satisfy more than one. To take the extreme example, *Macbeth*, 'The Scottish Play', is for our purposes a Scottish text.

The criteria are that the text:

1. makes some use of Scots language forms, e.g. 'The Maker to Posterity', *Sunset Song*, *The Pardoner's Tale*, *The Yellow on the Broom*;

2. uses Scottish literary forms, e.g. 'The Flyting between Montgomerie and Polwart', 'The Baron of Brackley', 'Elegy on Lucky Wood in the Canongate', 'Holy Willie's Prayer';

3. deals centrally with Scottish topics or aspects of life and is set in Scotland past or present, though the writer is not necessarily a Scot, e.g. *Confessions of a Justified Sinner*; *The Brave Days*; 'To Suffie, Last of the Buchan Fishwives'; *The Cheviot, the Stag and the Black, Black Oil*;

4. does not itself have an obvious Scottish dimension but emerges from an œuvre which does, e.g. *Ivanhoe*, *The Silverado Squatters*, *Peter Pan*, 'The First Men on Mercury';

5. has no obvious Scottish dimension but the writer was born or educated or lived in Scotland, e.g. 'The Vision of Judgement', *My First Summer in the Sierra*, *Richard of Bordeaux*, *Penelope's Hat*;

6. is from another literature but translated into some form of
Scots e.g. Belli's sonnets (Garioch), 'Luke's Gospel' (from *New
Testament in Scots*, Lorimer), *Tartuffe* (Lochhead).

Some would wish to go further and proclaim a number of themes as
sufficiently prominent in our literature to make them defining
characteristics of Scottishness – for example, preoccupations with the
domineering patriarch, with the devil, with attitudes to the land, with
the common folk or with dualisms of all kinds. We can safely assume,
however, that a wider review of other literatures would show that these
concerns are not so peculiarly Scottish as we may fondly suppose. We
walk a fine line between claiming for ourselves too little and too much.

On the vexed issue of the literary quality of Scottish materials, it is
worth noting that the American critic Leonard Bloom in his
idiosyncratic attempt to catalogue a Western canon[3] of the most important works of European and American literature includes eighteen
major authors whose writing qualifies as Scottish by our criteria. They
are Dunbar, Boswell, Smollett, Burns, Scott, Byron, Galt, Hogg,
Carlyle, James Thomson, John Davidson, Stevenson, George
Macdonald, David Lindsay, Muir, Norman Douglas, G. D. Brown,
MacDiarmid.

Our use of the expressions 'Scots' and 'Scots language forms' may
seem to beg the questions, 'Is there a Scots language? Was there ever
one? Is there one today?' These are matters of keen linguistic debate,
much depending on how one defines a self-standing language, but we
take the pragmatic view of the recent *Cambridge Encyclopedia of the English Language* that in practice there exists 'a well established use of the
label, the "Scots language" and a spirited defence of all that such a label
stands for.'[4] We do not, however, consider the use of Scots forms a
necessary condition for a work to be classed as Scottish. It is part of the
richness of our situation that our literature has spoken in many
tongues, from the sixteenth-century 'Inglis' of Dunbar to the
'Southron' of Boswell and the subtly shifting language choices of Burns
and Scott; from the Doric of William Alexander to the Gaelic
modulations of Neil Munro; from the urban demotic of Tom Leonard
to the mannered Standard of Candia McWilliam. For more detailed
discussion of language varieties in Scottish literature see the language
chapters of this volume and also Chapter 1 of *Language and Scottish
Literature*.[5]

CHOOSING TEXTS FOR SCHOOL USE

For school purposes the essential core of Scottish literature can be assumed to comprise works which substantially satisfy the first two or three of our criteria, e.g. 'The Fox and the Wolf', 'The Thrie Estaits', 'The Twa Corbies', 'The Daft Days', 'Tam o' Shanter', 'The Lady of the Lake', *Annals of the Parish*, *My Schools and Schoolmasters*, 'Drumdelgie', *Kidnapped*, *Open the Door!*, *Witch Wood*, *Wild Harbour*, *Mr Bolfry*, 'Hallaig' (in translation), 'Farewell to Sicily', *Linmill Stories*, 'Ikey on the People of Hellya', *Two Worlds*, *The Busconductor Hines*, 'Mirror's Song', *The Thoughts of Murdo* and *Bondagers*. It is likely that any course containing Scottish literature will rely heavily on materials of this kind. On the periphery, however, are texts which probably meet only one of the criteria, e.g. *Journey to the Western Islands of Scotland*, 'The Solitary Reaper', 'So we'll go no more a roving', *Treasure Island*, *The Admirable Crichton*, 'Bagpipe Music', *Private Angelo*. Some writers of children's fiction, such as R. M. Ballantyne and Rosemary Sutcliff, fall, for their different reasons, into this category. Course planners are likely to differ widely in their view and use of these marginal materials, but a generous, balanced view of the corpus will certainly find some place for writers of the diaspora such as Smollett, Boswell, Byron, Barrie, Buchan and Alastair Reid. Obviously it does the case no good to make absurd claims of annexation for intriguing offshore items such as *The Wind in the Willows* or *Peter Rabbit*. Between the heartland and the wilder fringes, however, lies a vast and diverse range of materials which may reasonably be defined in our terms as 'Scottish'. Within these admittedly debatable bounds there is no shortage of resources to sustain the study of Scottish literature at all levels in Scottish primary and secondary schools and institutions, whatever course arrangements are likely to prevail. Back in 1972, in his seminal essay 'The Resources of Scotland', Edwin Morgan mused upon the possible extent of our literature and surely struck the right note when he hoped that:

> The inclusiveness of 'yes', whatever the risk of accusations of chauvinism, would be preferred to the pedantry of 'no' ...[6]

FOR YOUNGER CHILDREN

Later chapters of this book will make recommendations for Scottish materials suitable for the various stages of the primary and secondary school. However, it is worth underlining at this point that one of the neglected but distinctive strengths of Scottish literature is the great wealth of texts it offers to younger children, in the 5–14 range. These include, for example:

1. popular rhymes of the kind collected by Chambers and the Montgomeries, with an attractive recent selection by Dunlop and Kamm;
2. traditional folk and fairy tales published in numerous anthologies such as: *Scottish Folk Tales and Legends* (Ker Wilson); *The Mouth of the Night* (Macfarlane), *A Forgotten Heritage* (Aitken), *A Cuckoo's Nest* and *A Scent of Water* (both MacDougall), *The Green Man of Knowledge* (Bruford), *The King of the Black Art* (Douglas), *A Kist of Whistles* (Miller), *Fireside Tales of the Traveller Children* and *Tales of the Seal People* (both Williamson), *Exodus to Alford* (Robertson), *Scottish Tales* and *The Goose Girls of Eriska* (both Blair), *Scottish Traditional Tales* (Bruford and MacDonald), *Penguin Book of Scottish Folk Tales* (Philip);
3. anthologies of poetry, songs, riddles, games and lore such as : *A Scots Kist* (The Burns Federation), *Ram Tam Toosh* (Macdonald and Brison), *Scotscape* (Hendry and Stephen), *A Scottish Poetry Book* (Bold), *The Minister's Cat* (Whyte and Robertson), *Gweed Gear Sma Buik* (Taylor and Wheeler);
4. poetry written for children by R. L. Stevenson, William Soutar, Sandy Thomas Ross, J. C. Milne, J. K. Annand, Sheena Blackhall;
5. a vast range of fiction written for children by, for example, George MacDonald, R. M. Ballantyne, Andrew Lang, R. L. Stevenson, J. M. Barrie, John Buchan, Naomi Mitchison, George Mackay Brown, Rosemary Sutcliff, Allan Campbell MacLean, Kathleen Fidler, Mollie Hunter, Iona McGregor, Joan Lingard, David Thomson, Eileen Dunlop, Frances Hendry, Donald Lightwood, Mairi Hedderwick;
6. fictional and autobiographical writing about childhood, often highly localised, which is readily accessible to younger readers in selected passages from writers such as J. J. Bell, Jessie Kesson, Mollie Weir, Finlay MacDonald and Betsy Whyte.

The abiding appeal of some of the traditional materials mentioned above has been demonstrated in recent years by popular children's entertainments such as Fisher and Tresize's 'Singing Kettle' shows and Communicado Theatre Company's *Tall Tales for Cold Dark Nights*.

BURNS FOR YOUNGER CHILDREN

In addition to sources such as those listed above, teachers can find rich
ample reserves of Scottish materials which were not consciously
written for or about children. Many of our best contemporary writers
yield opportunities, but perhaps the outstanding instance remains the
work of Burns. Some of his songs and his smaller pieces, as well as
extracts from the major poems, have the humour, rhythm and linguistic
playfulness that children love, particularly if there is also opportunity
for music. Burns himself said of one of them:

> 'Duncan Gray' is that kind of light-horse gallop of an air, which
> precludes sentiment. – The ludicrous is its ruling feature.[7]

Likely items include: 'Up in the Morning Early', 'Wee Willie Gray',
'Hey ca thro', 'We're a Noddin', 'O Whistle and I'll Come to ye my
Lad', 'Duncan Gray', 'To A Haggis', 'To a Louse', 'Address to the
Tooth-ache', 'O Willie Brew'd a Peck o' Maut', 'The Deil's Awa wi the
Exciseman', 'On Tam the Chapman', 'Killiecrankie', 'What will I do
gin my Hoggie Die?', 'Poor Mailie's Elegy', 'The Auld Man's Mare's
Dead', 'On a Schoolmaster in Cleish Parish', 'The Kirkcudbright
Grace'. Nor should we forget the wonderfully lively Scots prose tale of
'The Marriage of Robin Redbreast and the Wren' which according to
Burns's sister he made and told for the amusement of the younger
members of the family.

SOURCES OF ADVICE ON TEXTS

Some useful guidance on choosing and teaching suitable Scottish
materials for secondary students is to be found in the following
documents:

1. *Scottish Literature in the Secondary School* (SCCE, 1976) Published
   twenty years ago and obsolete in some of its educational
   references and assumptions, this pioneering report still has real
   value as a systematic survey of materials in different genres and
   of teaching approaches suitable for the various stages of the
   secondary school. Its exemplars are well worth considering and
   its book lists, while dated, yield much useful information. It
   contains an important essay by A. J. Aitken on the Scots
   language and the English teacher, which, though formally an
   appendix, is really the tail that wags the whole volume.

2. *Scottish Literature in the New Higher* (SCCC, 1989)   This document makes a strong case for the advantages of using Scottish materials in the Higher Grade English course. It contains many helpful suggestions for suitable texts, themes and groupings. Its main strength is a series of very practical teaching units and essays dealing in varying detail with writers appropriate for the Higher stage.

3. *Scottish Literature in the Upper Secondary School* (ASLS, 1992) Designed to augment and supplement the preceding volume, this reviews the range of materials, particularly more recent texts, suitable for Higher and Sixth Year Studies courses. It offers commentary and suggestions for discussion, and is notable for the attention which it gives to women writers. It has a select list of reference and critical works, audio cassettes, Scottish language studies and useful addresses.

4. *Effective Learning and Teaching in Scottish Secondary Schools* (SOED, 1992)   This Scottish Office Education Department report is important because it gives official backing to the idea that there is a canon of pre-twentieth-century 'Scottish works of quality' which should be drawn upon in English courses at all stages. It cites in evidence thirty-one authors, including the anonymous ballads and folk tales.

PLANNING COURSES

In school courses and examination syllabuses, as we have already noted, Scottish literature and language are implicitly treated as a subset of English literature and language. Most universities, it is true, now offer separate Scottish courses, but for a number of reasons – including pressures on the curriculum – substantial free-standing courses are not likely to materialise in the school sectors in the foreseeable future. In this document we therefore assume that in schools Scottish texts will for the most part be used within English courses, and that these courses will combine the study of language and literature. Planning and decision-making for secondary English courses legitimately takes place at different levels:

1. the government can issue national curricular guidance;
2. examining bodies such as SEB and SCOTVEC or a future joint group can define a syllabus;
3. individual school departments can agree course features;

4. individual teachers can make some decisions about texts and methods;
5. individual students can have some scope to choose texts and areas of study.

Across these levels the balance between definitive guidance and freedom of choice will always be problematic in English. We have to live with the fact that literature and language involve value systems which impinge upon living issues of morality, politics and religion. The press in Scotland from time to time highlights disputes about allegedly unsuitable books being used in examination courses or stocked in school libraries. Not surprisingly, these are often works which are on the cutting edge of contemporary writing and may be evidence of its vigour. In these circumstances who is best fitted to decide which texts are to be studied by young people? Should texts professed for examinations be prescribed, recommended or left to the discretion of individual teachers and students? Clearly national curricular and assessment agencies have a responsibility to define in general terms the field of desirable study, but this duty has to be reconciled as far as possible with the interests of parents, and the rights of teachers and students to pick texts suited to their own needs and interests.

We suggest that the Scottish dimension to the subject 'English' is a related issue which calls for central policy-making. The time has surely come for national curricular and assessment policy to guarantee a representation of the major Scottish texts. There are numerous precedents for such an approach: in all secondary schools in England students must now make some study of Shakespeare; in Italy they encounter Dante, in France Molière and in Germany Goethe. There is a strong case for insisting upon some similar, basic, national specification at the senior stages in Scotland, drawing perhaps upon Henryson, Dunbar, the ballads, Burns, Hogg, Scott, Stevenson, Bridie and MacDiarmid. This approach is compatible with safeguarding reasonable choice for teachers and students.

We believe that at whatever level course planning decisions are made for English in the secondary school, the following principles should be carefully observed:

1. There should be a good balance between Scottish texts and texts from English literatures.
2. In the choice of Scottish texts:
   (a) women writers should be present as well as men;
   (b) contemporary and earlier works should both have a place;
   (c) there should be a variety of genres;

(d) there should be a variety of Scottish and English language forms;

(e) there should be some scope for reference to other aspects of Scottish life and culture, namely music, art, history;

(f) there should be place for at least one Scottish media text (film, TV, radio, press).

3. Students should undertake imaginative writing using Scottish materials as stimuli and models, and have the opportunity to use appropriate forms of Scots language.

4. They should have the opportunity to meet contemporary Scottish writers.

5. They should have a chance to see a Scottish play in performance.

These recommended principles may seem too difficult to implement fully given timetabling constraints on English in secondary schools. If, however, they are applied to whole courses which stretch over two sessions (S1/S2; S3/S4; S5/S6) they may turn out to be manageable. At any rate they are worth arguing for and working towards.

USING SCOTTISH TEXTS

Some Fruitful Approaches

For the most part teachers at all stages will present Scottish items in the same ways as they would any other literary materials. They are likely to select approaches (whole-class, group, individual) which are suited to their lesson aims and to the needs and interests of their students at that time, rather than because of any supposed Scottish characteristics of the texts.

Good practice in teaching literature in Scottish schools was surveyed in 1992 in a report by HM Inspectors of Schools.[8] Generally the methods described there apply as well to Scottish as to other texts. The impact of current literary theory on teaching is discussed elsewhere in this volume but it is worth noting here that one of the most productive techniques emerging in English classrooms over recent years originated in an influential strategy for text-based workshops set out in 1987 by Durant and Fabb, then of the University of Strathclyde.[9] In their recommended investigative activities students engage closely with texts in language assignments which comprise comparison, replacement, ordering, completion, prediction, classification, problem-solving, continuation, composition and performance. Some of these tasks are of value at any stage, depending on the choice of text; others are probably best suited to the more advanced secondary courses.

Since Scottish literature coexists with the major literatures of English and has been greatly influenced by them, and since its texts range widely across English and Scots language forms, some of these workshop techniques which involve forms of comparison turn out to be particularly valuable. Pairings are worth considering between Scottish texts and English texts on similar topics, or between texts in different dialects; between Scots and English versions of a text; between English and Scots language forms within the same text. For example, at the earlier stages in poetry a comparison can be made of De la Mare's 'The Little Green Orchard' and Soutar's 'Bawsy Broon'; for middle stage secondary in prose, 'Sredni Vashtar' ('Saki') and 'The Cat' (McLellan); for more advanced stages in drama, *Dancing at Lughnasa* (Friel) and *The Steamie* (Roper). Among composition and other responsive activities there is value in assignments which call for continuing, completing or translating texts in Scots and English or in different dialect forms.

Our Scottish corpus of literature is relatively less well supplied in drama than in the other main genres, but that does not mean that text-based dramatic activities need be neglected. There is some benefit to be had at all stages in using assignments whose aim is to transform poems and prose into dramatic pieces. In the past, teachers have sensibly exploited some of the better known ballads in this way, for example 'Sir Patrick Spens', 'The Wife of Usher's Well' and 'Get up and Bar the Door'. Many exciting dramatic possibilities also exist among traditional tales to be found in *The Green Man of Knowledge* and the other collections listed earlier.

Though it would be misleading to claim certain themes as exclusively Scottish, nonetheless our literature is particularly fertile in some areas of human experience and less so in others. Warfare, encounters with the supernatural, the world of animals, seafaring, travel and exile are a few groupings that come readily to mind. These enable students to explore conjunctions of attitudes and styles. Such groupings can be developed across the genres to include good non-fictional items.

If, as we urge, the teaching of Scottish literature is satisfactorily resourced, there will also be opportunities to enrich learning by enlisting appropriate art and music, through contacts with the local community and visits by Scottish writers and by seeing Scottish plays in performance.

SOME OBSTACLES

We have already suggested the advantages which Scottish materials have to offer. It is worth considering finally whether there are any particular obstacles to their use. In 1976 the SCCC report on Scottish literature in the secondary school identified four features of these materials which may present difficulties to many teachers:

1. they show a preoccupation with the national past;
2. they are mostly concerned with the rural rather than the urban scene;
3. the bulk are strongly localised, but some localities are poorly represented;
4. in some texts the Scots language may cause problems for students.[10]

These features might be thought to render Scots texts in some ways irrelevant to young people's interests, but the report sees them as challenges which are worthwhile since the texts offer vitality of language and illumination of experience which remain valuable for young Scots today.

INDIFFERENCE

In the twenty years since the report was published indifference to Scottish culture has certainly diminished, but it remains true that in some places teachers may still encounter resistance among students and their parents (and even among colleagues) on the grounds that they are selling students short by including Scottish items in the English curriculum. The charge is that Scottish texts are second-rate and parochial and are sometimes crudely offensive in tone, and that Scots language forms are simply a *déclassé* form of English, useless in the wider world. Individual enthusiastic teachers can, through the example of their own teaching, do something to overcome the obstacle of such prejudices but they need backup. Fortunately English departments can now in their communications with parents explain that there is clear official support for Scottish literature and language in national curricular guidance and examination syllabuses. There is no danger that students will be disadvantaged through studying Scottish materials; on the contrary, they are more likely to benefit academically.

Our primary schools have a crucial role to play in cultivating and naturalising these studies. It is important that they should take up the very positive encouragement given in the national guidelines on English Language 5–14 and ensure that the teaching of Scottish literature and language develops progressively from the earliest stages.[11] They should also be helped to explore the opportunities for Scottish studies suggested by the corresponding guidelines on Environmental Studies and the Expressive Arts. If the confident use of Scottish materials is established early on in school, there is less likelihood that prejudice will remain an obstacle in the future.

RESOURCES

Poor resourcing can also prove a major restriction upon methods of teaching. Primary schools and secondary departments which wish to use Scottish materials need to build up their stocks of resources. These holdings should contain not only class or group sets of texts but also single copies for class and school libraries, dictionaries and other reference works in language and literature, critical texts, key background books on Scottish history, music and art, and also audio-visual resources related to these areas of interest.

Schools can claim with some justice to be chronically underfunded for most aspects of the curriculum, but the difficulties are compounded for Scottish studies because these areas do not usually have existing fallback reserves of materials. Moreover, some good texts are permanently out of print or go in and out of print with bewildering speed. Sadly, for example, most of the publications listed above as suitable for younger children are not presently available. Scottish publishers should not be blamed for these problems. They have in the past shown themselves ready to respond to curricular developments, but the potential market is small and as commercial ventures they cannot be expected to subsidise the education system. It seems that excellent series such as Canongate Classics and Kelpies have survived at best only precariously. Unless schools are in a position to invest substantially, we cannot realistically hope to see in print the kinds of materials which this book is promoting or to achieve an enterprising repertoire of teaching methods. Admittedly teachers can do a certain amount by judicious legal photocopying. Although this recourse may help with brief items such as poems and short stories, it is no good with novels or drama. For classroom purposes it is a poor second-best since the copies generally turn out to be shabby, short-lived and expensive. Determined teachers manage to overcome some of the obstacles of inadequate resourcing, but we have no right to expect it of them as a matter of course.

If the claims made in this chapter are to have any chance of being realised, we need to revive nationally the efforts made in the past to maintain in print a substantial core of Scottish literature for use in schools. Recently the Scottish Consultative Council on the Curriculum has joined with the publisher Nelson Blackie to produce a stimulating anthology of texts mostly in Scottish dialects and Gaelic. The collection, which is accompanied by a useful range of ancillary materials, is designed for students in the 5–14 age range. The resulting *Kist/A' Chiste* is an optimistic step in the right direction.

NOTES

1. SCCE, *Scottish Literature in the Secondary School* (Edinburgh: HMSO, 1976), p. 5.
2. T. S. Eliot's (1919) review, 'Was there a Scottish Literature?' is quoted in P. Crotty, 'Keeping no southern', *Times Literary Supplement*, 11 August 1995, pp. 3, 4.
3. Leonard Bloom, *The Western Canon* (London: Macmillan, 1995), pp. 531–67.
4. David Crystal, *The Cambridge Encyclopedia of the English Language* (Cambridge, 1995), p. 328.
5. J. Corbett (ed.), *Language and Scottish Literature*, Scottish Language and Literature series, Volume 2 (EUP, 1997).
6. Edwin Morgan, collected in *Essays* (Cheadle: Carcanet, 1974), pp. 158–65.
7. *The Letters of Robert Burns*, Volume 11, edited by J. D. Ferguson and R. Roy (Oxford, 1985), pp. 163–4.
8. SOED, *Effective Learning and Teaching in Scottish Secondary Schools: English* (Edinburgh: SOED, 1992), pp. 37, 38.
9. Alan Durant and Nigel Fabb, *The Linguistics of Writing* (Manchester: Manchester University Press, 1987), pp. 232–4.
10. SCCE, *Scottish Literature in the Secondary School* (Edinburgh: HMSO, 1976), p. 5.
11. SOED, *National Guidelines: English Language 5–14* (Edinburgh: SOED, 1991).
12. SCCC, *The Kist/A' Chiste* (Edinburgh: Nelson Blackie, 1996).

EXEMPLAR 5

Level/stage of school

S1/2.

Duration

2 periods plus.

Topic/text(s)

Dramatisation of a ballad: 'The Wife of Usher's Well' (Anon.).

Purposes

To encourage pupils' imaginative thinking and dramatic expressiveness by exploring a traditional ballad.

To make pupils aware of the essentially dramatic structure of the ballad and of the narrative power contained in a compressed narrative.

Teaching approaches

1. Supply the pupils with copies of the ballad 'The Wife of Usher's Well'. Read the ballad and discuss the story (focusing on the sequence of events: the sending off of the brothers to trade abroad, the two messages about the loss at sea – rumour and confirmation, the mother's (witch's) curse upon the elements, the continuing raging storms, the return of the brothers from the troubled sea, the signs that they have returned from the dead, their arrival home and their mother's welcome, the feast with the brothers' probable reaction to it, the retiral to bed with the mother's vigil at the bedside, the coming of dawn and the cocks' crowing, the dialogue of the brothers, their departure, the waking of the mother and her reactions to her final loss).

2. Work out the sequence of scenes; pupils in groups discuss and improvise their own versions of particular sequences of scenes, sharing out the different parts (three brothers, mother-witch, messengers, lass kindling fire, assorted servants and sailors, raging sea and winds, red and grey cocks, etc.).

3. Conclude with a complete run-through of the ballad-play.

Products

The worked-out drama as an imaginative entity.

Accompanying notes.

Follow-up writing as desired.

Supporting Materials

There are good drama textbooks and guides for teachers, e.g. *The Group Approach to Drama* (Adland).

Other comments

Traditional Scottish ballads lend themselves well to dramatic treatment, which is a good way into the basic story and tone of a ballad, and also requires a concentration on the hidden elements of the story (those parts that are leapt over and understood by the hearers as having happened). There are, of course, other elements requiring to be discussed.

EXEMPLAR 6

Level/stage of school

S4/5.

Duration

1/2 periods.

Topic/text(s)

Extract on 'Macbeth' from John Bellenden's translation of *The Chronicles of Scotland* complied by Hector Boece; *Macbeth* by William Shakespeare.

Purposes

To examine an old Scottish historical text and find parallels and differences between it and Shakespeare's *Macbeth*, showing that Shakespeare's source derives from Scottish writing.

Teaching approaches

1. Language work: reading of text together; use of glossary and/or *Concise Scots Dictionary*; discussion of obscure expressions; identification of Scots usages (e.g. 'quh-' pronoun forms); annotation of printed text.

2. Literature work: identification (in group discussion) of dialogue in the play *Macbeth* parallel to references in the Scots text; identification of major differences between the texts.

Products

Sheet with corresponding parallel texts (Shakespearean dialogue and Scots prose) in two-column format.

Annotated Scots text for future reference.

Supporting materials

Concise Scots Dictionary (for reference).

Teacher's prepared glossary of text.

Texts of *Macbeth*.

Other comment

More of the Scots chronicle text about MacBeth can be found in Bellenden. Another Scots chronicle (in verse) is *Chronica Gentis Scotorum* by John of Fordun (Scottish Texts Society). It also contains the story of MacBeth. A more fanciful treatment of MacBeth appears in Andrew of Wyntoun's *Orygynale Cronykil* (Scottish Texts Society).

EXEMPLAR 7

Level/stage of school

S6.

Duration

As determined by teacher.

Topic/text(s)

A major Scottish play: 'Ane Plesaunt Satyre of the Thrie Estaitis' by Sir David Lyndsay.

Purposes

To experience a major Scottish Renaissance dramatic text that still influences the Scottish theatre.

To observe how drama can be a vehicle for strong political and social criticism.

Teaching approaches

1. *Preliminary work by teacher* Read the play carefully with the help of Lyall's notes and other criticism; decide how to divide the play into scenes and distinct episodes for ease of pupil study; prepare a text for pupils, preferably a double spread with dialogue on the left hand page and space for pupils' notes on the right-hand page alongside the text.

2. Given the maturity of the pupils studying the play, the work will be done best in independent groups with the teacher acting as adviser. The pupils might be given the notional task of preparing a presentation of the play, so they have to discuss the flow of the action, the characterisation, the staging and setting. To do this, they have to read the play cooperatively and work out any difficulties they encounter. They should report their progress at regular intervals to keep on course.

3. The work should culminate in a major seminar in which they brief the supposed director and actors of the play on the comedy, the satire and the political messages, etc.

Products

Pupils' annotated copies of text.

Briefing folders containing the groups' findings on the play and their recommendations to the actors and director.

Taped readings of sections.

Supporting materials

Scots dictionaries.
Background material on David Lyndsay, the Scotland of James V, the Three
Estates (or Parliament), the causes of the Reformation in Scotland, etc
Information about the staging of early drama in the open air on holidays and
festivals.

Other comments

There is no avoiding the fact that this is a very difficult text, presenting a challenge
in language and ideas. This, however, should make the effort worthwhile.

EXEMPLAR 8

Level/stage of school

S4.

Duration

5 periods.

Topic/text(s)

Study of the 'Standard Habbie' verse form: 'The Life and Death of Habbie
Simpson, the Piper of Kilbarchan' (Robert Sempill of Beltrees); 'The Last Dying
Words of Bonnie Heck, a Famous Greyhound in the Shire of Fife' (William
Hamilton of Gilbertfield); 'Elegy on Lucky Wood in the Canongate' (Allan
Ramsay); 'Braid Claith' and 'To the Tron-Kirk Bell' (Robert Fergusson).

Purposes

To introduce pupils to a very popular verse form in Scottish poetry, and to
prepare the way for a more extended study of poems by Robert Burns.

To show the range of uses and tones that can be expressed in the same
verse form.

Teaching approaches

1. The poems (with any others desired by the teacher) should be taught in the normal way, perhaps with only a single period devoted to each. An appreciation of the range and variety of the poems is more important than an exhaustive examination of each in depth.

2. The basic form should be analysed with its two rhymes and use of four eight-syllable lines with four stresses varied with two four-syllable lines with two stresses.

3. The variety of uses and tones shown in the poems is the main concern of the teaching: how it moves from being an elegy form lamenting a death to being more satirical or comic while still being elegiac, until it moves away from the elegy purpose to being a general form for satire, comedy, celebration, etc. This will prepare for the very wide range of uses which Burns demonstrates. A question to ask is: does the stanza form itself with its short lines, tripping metre and clinching last line operate against a very serious extended use of the form, and does it tend naturally towards humour? Examination of the tone and purpose will automatically bring up the question of language: the use of Scots language needs to be examined and discussed.

Products

Pupils' and teacher's notes.

Any writing set as follow-up.

Supporting materials

Concise Scots Dictionary and/or *Pocket Scots Dictionary*

Other comments.

This topic is also useful for putting Burns into a clear tradition of vernacular Scots writing.

EXEMPLAR 9

Level/stage of school

S5.

Duration

2 periods.

Topic/text(s)

Study of a Burns poem: 'The Twa Dogs'.

Purposes

To make pupils aware of a satirical technique in writing which uses a dialogue of detached commentators to highlight social ills.

To give pupils a good literary text for possible examination purposes.

Teaching approaches

1. Supply pupils with texts, on double-spread sheets with text on left-hand side and space for pupils' notes on the right.

2. Read poem (or listen to good taped reading with two or three voices); discuss the form of poem (dialogue between two dogs with different social backgrounds, bringing out examples of social class injustice and abuse of privilege and money). Refer to the pastoral convention and the eclogue form, in which shepherds discuss matters of interest, which may be the follies of artificial society set against their own simple natural lives. Note how Caesar is the critic of the rich landed gentry, while Luath (based on Burns's own sheepdog) is conditioned to know his place and respect his betters.

3. Pupils discuss and make notes about the respective views of the dogs: the realities exposed by Caesar and the illusions that Luath clings to. Consider finally how outspoken or revolutionary this poem is; note it belongs to c. 1785, four years before the French Revolution. Is Burns treading a fine line between making strong social criticism and avoiding giving offence to potential subscribers to his Kilmarnock Edition of Poems? Does the use of dogs as critics (in the old tradition of using animals as intelligent commentators) deflect some of the possible hostile reaction while keeping the bite of the criticism?

4. The work on the poem can be rounded off with a critical essay on the poem written by pupils to practise the kind of academic writing required by the external examinations.

Products

Pupils'·essays on the poem.
Pupils' annotated copies of poems for future reference.

Supporting materials

Background material as desired on eighteenth-century aristocratic and peasant life, the Grand Tour, etc.

Reproductions of eighteenth- and early nineteenth century paintings, for example idealised portraits of aristocratic families set against satirical works like Hogarth's *The Rake's Progress* sequence or a realistic work like Wilkie's *Distraining for Rent*.

A good biography of Burns for reference.

Other comments

There is a wealth of useful classroom material in the area of Scottish art. The main galleries in Glasgow and Edinburgh have many postcards and prints of Scottish paintings that can tie in directly with Scottish texts of different periods, as well as being the stimulus for original work in writing and talk.

Part II Scottish Language

3

LANGUAGE IN SCOTLAND TODAY

George Sutherland

INTRODUCTION

There has been in recent decades an undeniable upsurge in the study of Scottish literature in both schools and universities in Scotland. While the uptake is not consistent across the whole of Scotland, the situation no doubt reflects the increasing confidence of growing numbers of teachers and a burgeoning interest among students. This raises a number of interesting questions, not all of which have satisfactory answers. Perhaps we are too close to the questions to be able to provide the answers as yet. Some of the questions are addressed elsewhere in this series of volumes, but one which is of enduring concern yet is evaded as a matter of course, it seems, is: What of the Scots language in which much of that literature is written? There is a clear disjunction. While the literature is now seen (admittedly after a long period of neglect and official disapproval) as a formalised and recognisable discipline, for the language there is no agreed standard approach and no shared vision.

It is time that there was.

It has first to be stated firmly that, in objective linguistic terms, Scots is a language like any other, with its own structure, its own literature, its own set of varieties. It is also a language cognate with English. It is definitely not a debased form of English. Neither is it completely independent of English, nor, for that matter, is English entirely independent of Scots.

THE DEVELOPMENT OF SCOTS

Both Scots and English are derived from a core Germanic language brought to these islands by the invading Anglian and Saxon peoples. The language of the Anglian settlers in the northern parts (i.e. later

Lothian and the Eastern Borders) was affected by other invaders from the Norse lands, and this Anglo-Danish speech in turn was affected much later by other continental influences. The language that is now called Scots evolved from these origins and flourished as an official language between the opening of the twelfth and the beginning of the eighteenth centuries. The Saxon, or Old English, language that has become English was subject to rather different influences, very significantly from Norman French. By the fifteenth century, Scots (or, as it was then rather confusingly called, 'Inglis', to distinguish it from the much older Gaelic, or 'Scottis', language it had gradually and largely displaced to the northern and western parts of Scotland) had reached a high level of sophistication and was the language of court and commerce and of daily intercourse. It was also the language of intellectual discourse and literature. Latin was the language of extreme formality, the Church, higher education and international exchange. English ('Southron') was the language of another country, England.

We all know what happened next, for it is the subject of the enduring and endearing lament so close to the hearts of many self-conscious Scots, the keening and grieving which is actually a form of satisfaction and a vindication of their position – that is, the celebration of the lost cause, the romantic failure. Several important factors intervened, and collectively, cumulatively, they brought Scots to its present position, one of the three languages of Scotland – but, for many linguistic purposes, not always the predominant one.

The factors which brought about this linguistic situation in Scotland are well-known. These factors were, first, the Reformation and the decision to bring the Christian message to ordinary people in the vernacular rather than in the Latin of the Vulgate. After a number of Scots and English attempts, the official vernacular version that was finally offered in both Scotland and England was, for understandable economic and political reasons, the English. That is one of the reasons for English to this day being perceived as the 'Attic' language, the hieratic high-status language as opposed to the 'Doric' language of the Scots 'hoi polloi'. Every time people speak sentimentally about the guid auld Scots Doric, they perpetuate this classically inspired false social distinction.

The second determinant was the decision of the Scottish king, James VI, when he succeeded to the English throne as James I, to establish his court in the capital of his new rich southern kingdom rather than in Edinburgh. The pressures on James personally and on his Scots nobility to adopt English for formal purposes became irresistible and filtered down through all ranks of educated Scottish society. This cultural phenomenon, the adoption of the language of the court and the consequent reductive effect on the alternative popular language, however powerful it may have been, can be traced without difficulty in almost every civilisation.

Finally, the political union of the two kingdoms in 1707 consolidated the process that had begun a century and a half before by removing the Scottish legislature to the English capital. The several eighteenth-century revolts against the monarchy that followed that union, supported by much of the Gaelic-speaking Highlands, led to the virtual extirpation and certainly the marginalisation of the Gaelic culture and language.

Subsequent history has done a great deal to endorse the situation that was created during the eighteenth century and accounts for the present relative status of the three languages. There have been further pressures, mainly social, political/economic and cultural, and many of them still apply. It is no exaggeration to say that these long-past events still echo on the Scottish linguistic situation, with continuing effects. Curiously, however, in contrast to the case of Gaelic, where suppression of the language was an explicit intention, the effects on the Scots language were probably unintentional, though devastating.

THE LANGUAGES OF SCOTLAND

The present sequence of chapters deals with different aspects of language in Scotland, notably with the three historical languages. The oldest of these traditional languages, Gaidhlig, 'the language of heaven' (pronounced 'Gahlic' and anglicised to 'Gaelic' – ironic that in its own land it is consistently misspelt and mispronounced), is today in a precarious position even in its remaining heartland of the north and west, despite official encouragement by means of broadcasting and some educational provision. Yet, paradoxically, in its literary output it is experiencing a kind of Renaissance.

English, in the variety known as Scottish Standard English, is the official language of modern Scotland and is understood, though not necessarily used, by virtually the whole population. For some Scots, it is their only language. Nobody can deny that the possession of this variety of English is a massive asset in the international context, yet it is conversely argued, with some passion, that the use of English is an inhibiting factor in situations of social class mingling and educational development. In historico-linguistic terms it is a parvenu, being the most recently introduced of the three languages.

The third traditional language, as we have seen, is Scots, the natural spoken language of the huge majority, about 80 per cent, of Scots people living in Lowland Scotland. It is the surviving form of the official language of the pre-Union Scottish kingdom, but this should not be construed as the beginning of an argument for its revival in that form.

Few Scots are monoglots: most are bilingual in English and Scots or Gaelic; trilingual ability in all three is rare. In this, unlike the monoglot English, Scots share in a widespread European experience of language. The Swiss are a case in point. While each of their languages has its natural home and the factors which determine the use of each normally allow them to sit easily together, there are areas where conflict occurs and where there is a clear struggle for dominance. The conflict in Scotland can be illustrated by an example familiar to all English teachers. Consider the language of much contemporary realistic Scottish fiction: Scots, often allied to a popular preference for strong language, comes from the page and conflicts with the linguistic gentility of an Anglicised bourgeoisie (professional parents and teachers). The social aspects of the language, the paralinguistics, always intrude. Middle-class objections to much of current Scots prose fiction usage seem to be more on grounds of social taste than of linguistic appropriateness.

The linguistic situation of Scots and of the Scots is not unique, despite a chauvinistic and popular belief that it is. Almost every other European country today has or has had in the very recent past an official language and at least one other coexisting with it. Think only of the examples of Spain, Ireland, Belgium, Italy, France. Many languages have had to be rescued from near-oblivion or artificially promoted to ensure their survival or their dominance: Erse had political and cultural reasons for survival; Nynorsk and Riksmal in Norway were still being developed in the twentieth century. Nationalism and independence fuelled the process of restoring the former languages of Norway and ousting the Danish that had overwhelmed them; English became the official language of the United States only after a serious debate about the possibility of adopting German; in England the Anglo-Saxon language (English) was almost totally eclipsed by Norman French for two hundred years. Events in Canada are fascinating and still developing. It is useful to speculate on the comparative linguistic situations in Wales and Ireland, who have had the same powerful neighbour as the Scots; it is, of course, too late for the Cornish and the Manx.

There is a growing realisation that some aspects of the language question are absurdities that can be explained only by the operation of what amounts to propaganda and disinformation. Why am I writing in English to advocate the study and use of Scots? Indeed, why should I be writing in Scotland with any need to promote Scots? In most countries there is an unsurprising assumption that the 'mother tongue' will be read, written, heard, spoken, taught and learned. It is salutary to consider those few countries, like Tibet, Kurdistan and Malaysian Borneo, where this assumption is not being implemented and to reflect upon the reasons for that.

It will be argued still by some that the same assumption holds in Scotland too and that it is in fact being fulfilled: that English is the mother tongue. Here and elsewhere in this volume that notion is largely rejected.

SCOTTISH LANGUAGE IN THE SCHOOLS

It is the task of philologists and linguistic specialists as well as literary critics to define and describe language theoretically. For the purposes of education we must go further. It is simply not going to be adequate to encourage the study of the language in which Scottish literature is largely written simply as if it were a dead language existing only in written form. For the promotion of the study and the writing of Scottish literature, there is a logical imperative to study the language in the four separate but interdependent modes in which it is used – reading, writing, talking and listening. Anyone familiar with the current situation of Scots in society will recognise a clear difficulty here. There is a vicious circle, and, as often happens, it is essential that the circle is broken in the schools, given some substantial help from outside.

It was remarked recently that the Scottish Education Department was now apologising for all the wrongs perpetrated by the educational system over the last few centuries. While it might not have explicitly repressed the Scots used by generations of pupils, it certainly did nothing or little to encourage it in the concern to provide an education in English. There is a poetic justice in the idea of a resurgence of Scots taking place in our schools; that is where it has fared very badly in the past. Given the popular perceptions of Scots as rooted in a deprived underclass, there is some irony in its support now in the schools, themselves often perceived as bastions of bourgeois values, gentility and no little hypocrisy. It is pleasing to report that recent surveys of teacher (not just English teacher) attitudes towards pupils who speak Scots indicate that there is less unthinking opposition.

Certain official bodies appear to be adopting a changed attitude to Scots. The Scottish Education Department (now the SOEID), the Scottish Examination Board and the Scottish Consultative Committee on the Curriculum are actively providing support for the promotion of Scots literature and language in a number of ways: financial and moral support for the Scots Language Society; production of *The Kist/A' Chiste*, the anthology of Scots and Gaelic writing, with associated teaching materials, to support language work in the 5–14 curriculum; the increasing promotion of Scottish literature in the examination system, particularly at Higher Grade and at CSYS, but increasingly also in Higher Still, both in Higher and in Advanced Higher proposals for the inclusion of literature and language studies in Scots. It is very significant that proposals for the compulsory study of Scottish literature (for the first time since the introduction of the Higher over a century ago) have met with no real resistance, except, perhaps predictably in view of the social overtones of language, from a few independent schools. At the university level, we now have not only Scottish texts being studied and Scottish courses to contain them, but an increasing number of professorial chairs in Scottish literature.

This volume is intended to encourage both Scottish literary study and linguistic study of the three languages of Scotland as used in the literature. The timing is opportune and there is a pragmatic strategy in place for the study of Scottish language. Public interest in the languages of Scotland is attested by a number of straws blowing in the wind of change. When we see the media paying more regular attention to Scottish language matters, from advertising campaigns for whisky and tabloid newspapers to serious programmes and features, something is happening. The success of publications in Scots like Lorimer's *New Testament in Scots* and Jamie Stuart's 'Gospels in Scots', serious and humorous books about Glasgow dialect like *The Patter*, a succession of Scots and Gaelic dictionaries, the most recent being the *Scots School Dictionary*, all indicate a growing public interest in their own forms of language. Even a widely reported and criticised rebuke of a witness by a foolhardy Sheriff for using 'Aye' rather than the English 'Yes' is a marker of change.

THE FUTURE

Of course, the future for Scots in our schools is tied to its future in public life and dependent on factors already suggested. Some of these seem almost simplistically to be the reversal of some of the historical causes of its present situation. The feasibility of this is totally untested. Other factors appear to be part of a strategy, conscious or not, that is already under way.

Conditions that will secure the place of Scots are:

1. official recognition of Scots, Gaelic and English as the equally valid languages of Scotland;
2. a framework established for a modern standard of Scots, supported by a new grammar and dictionary;
3. stronger support for the study of the Scots and Gaelic languages in schools, and an appropriate examination structure from the new qualifications authority.

These, with others yet to be raised and discussed in the context of impending constitutional/political change and the recognition of our multicultural society, would change things. The experiences of Norway in the twentieth century and of the English language in the Middle Ages encourage us to see that even a period of 350 years in the darkness may be no more than an incubation period, an interlude between acts. It may presage a new stert tae ane auld sang.

EXEMPLAR 10

Level/stage of school

Any stage as felt appropriate.

Duration

5 periods plus (as much as teacher feels necessary).

Topic/text(s)

A study of the different languages to be found in Scotland, leading to a public display or exhibition.

Purposes

To make pupils aware of the multilingual nature of Scottish society, both in the past and in the present.

To spread this awareness beyond the classroom (to the school, to parents, etc.).

Teaching approaches

1. Discuss with pupils the different languages they hear spoken around them in their everyday lives; list these for future consideration. Extend the discussion to include languages and dialects the pupils might hear if they moved to other parts of Scotland; list these also.

2. Collect examples in writing and on tape of as many of these languages as possible (from pupils, their parents and grandparents and neighbours, from newspapers, libraries, etc.). Discuss some of these examples with the class. Discuss how an exhibition or display might be set up to inform people about 'The Languages of and in Scotland' (the traditional languages, the more recently arrived languages, the languages of visitors and tourists, etc.).

3. Pupils in groups prepare exhibits for display (posters, texts, notices, maps, pictures, tapes, etc.), with each group being responsible for a different language (or group of languages).

4. Mount the exhibition in a suitable space in the school (e.g. library, hall) and/or for a particular occasion (e.g. parents' night, school open day) by arrangement with other staff.

Products

The exhibition/display itself.

Associated language examples (perhaps in folders).

Necessary writing for the organisation (letters to outside agencies or individuals, publicity material like notices for display inside and outside the school, etc.).

Audio-tapes of spoken language or songs.

Supporting materials

Exhibition stands.

Display boards.

Dictionaries of Scots, Gaelic, etc.

Other comments

This project should afford ample opportunities for liaison with other staff and outside bodies. There is also a valuable dimension of language education about Scots, Gaelic and English as distinct languages of Scotland.

EXEMPLAR 11

Level/stage of school

S3.

Duration

2 periods.

Topic/texts

A study of Scots proverbs and their application to real-life situations.

Purposes

To enable pupils to see that proverbs are part of popular culture and come out of everyday language and situations.

To give pupils opportunities to write creatively, using proverbs as the stimulus.

Teaching approaches

1. Prepare a set of about ten Scots proverbs, chosen for their linguistic effect and their applicability to life. Suitable sources include *Scots Saws* (David Murison) and *A Collection of Scots Proverbs*.

2. Distribute the set to groups and have pupils discuss their meaning and application to real-life situations; follow with whole-class discussion, putting pupils' ideas together.

3. Pupils write a moral tale applying the proverb to an invented situation, ending the story with the proverb as a moral. Writing may be in either Scots or English.

4. Collect the stories into booklets of moral or exemplary tales.

Products

Pupils' writings collected into booklets.

Supporting materials

A collection of Scots proverbs for teacher and pupil use

Copies of *Scots School Dictionary* or *Pocket Scots Dictionary*.

Other comments

This topic can be handled at any stage of the school. More can probably be made of the language and writing if it is treated as an early Standard Grade unit.

EXEMPLAR 12

Level/stage of school

S3/4.

Duration

2 periods.

Topic/text(s)

Development of creative writing out of an Older Scots prose text: 'Summons of the Doomed of Flodden', Robert Lindsay of Pitscottie.

Purposes

To introduce the pupils to an Older Scots text by a sixteenth-century historian, with its features of language.

To develop the imaginative potential of a mysterious story for pupils' creative writing.

Teaching approaches

1. Supply pupils with copies of the extract with its accompanying English version. Read the Scots text, following it on the parallel versions; discuss some of the language differences between the Scots and English versions (vocabulary, grammar, spelling, etc.).

2. Discuss the mysterious voice and its message of doom, how it might have come to be believed in after the disaster of Flodden, why it has been included in a work of history, etc.

3. Set up writing by the pupils on the topic – perhaps a retelling of the event from another person's point of view, Richard Lawson's account of it in later years, a newspaper feature on the ghostly voice, etc.

Products

The pupils' writings on the topic.

Supporting materials

Copies of the text.

A Scots dictionary for reference.

Other texts relating to the Battle of Flodden.

Other comments

A more ambitious piece of writing might arise out of the fact that the story has some of the qualities of a traditional ballad. After a reading of one or two ballads to give pupils an awareness of the ballad stanza form and some of the typical ballad language and techniques of repetition, there might be an attempt to write the story as a popular ballad.

EXEMPLAR 13

Level/stage of school

S3/4.

Duration

2 periods.

Topic/text(s)

'St Giles' Day Riot in Edinburgh': extract from *The History of the Reformation in Scotland*, John Knox.

Purposes

To read a Renaissance Scots text dealing with a critical moment in Scottish history.

To transfer its content into another more modern format (the radio news report) to highlight its contemporary relevance.

Teaching approaches

1. The pupils are supplied with copies of the prose extract and read it themselves first to gain a general impression of the episode; the extract can then be read in sections (corresponding to the sequence of main events) with accompanying discussion to identify the different factions (the Catholic Bishops and their followers; the Presbyterian Town Council and the 'brethren'; the French Queen Regent, a Catholic), and the events culminating in the street riot and the smashing of the saint's image. Discuss how the events of the text relate to modern examples of religious bigotry and hatred in Scotland and elsewhere.

2. The pupils in groups then discuss the making of a Radio Scotland news report of the riot (main report, interviews, background information); the scripts are written; recordings are made on audiotape. An ambitious extension of this would be a video report on camcorder.

Products

Annotated copies of the extract. Scripts for news report.

Recordings on audio or video.

Supporting materials

Audio or video recorder.

Background information on John Knox and the Reformation in Scotland.

Other comments

Tying this topic to a historical event long ago may be one way of taking the heat out of a discussion on such a sensitive issue for some areas of Scotland. It may also go some way towards showing pupils how the religious division came about and that it is not merely an Irish issue. There are many modern Scottish poems and stories on the topic of bigotry and violence that can be used to back it up if necessary.

4

·

GAELIC – THE SENIOR PARTNER

Ronald W. Renton

Scottish Gaelic belongs to the family of Celtic languages, the others being Breton, Welsh and Irish Gaelic. Breton and Welsh are known as P-Celtic languages and Irish and Scottish Gaelic as Q-Celtic languages. It is almost certain that forms of P-Celtic speech (including Pictish) were spoken throughout Scotland before Gaelic arrived as the language of immigrant settlers from Ireland in the late third and mid-fourth centuries. Gradually these immigrants, the Scots, increased in numbers and strength eventually to establish the colony of Dalriada, the name already used for their home area in the North of Ireland, in about AD 500. It was to this community that Columba came and in 563 he established Iona as his headquarters.

Argyll, which means 'the coastland of the Gael', became the new Gaelic kingdom and from it Gaelic spread out to become the language of most of Scotland, with the notable exceptions of Lothian and the eastern Borders as place name evidence will testify. It was most widely spoken from the tenth to the thirteenth centuries and began to contract slowly after this. That contraction was accelerated from about 1750 onwards – the aftermath of the Jacobite Rising of 1745 and the Industrial Revolution. It is now spoken by approximately only 1 per cent of the population and yet it commands a sympathy in the national consciousness far in excess of its physical survival. Many Scots have an awareness of their Gaelic past – of Columba and the Celtic Church, of Prince Charles Edward and the '45, of the Highland Clearances and many other such personalities and events. Despite some silly Lowland prejudices against Highlanders that can still occasionally be discerned, many Scots feel a strong direct link with it, their grandparents and great-grandparents having been Gaelic speakers.

Since, therefore, our Gaelic heritage is clearly important to us, our pupils are entitled to have some access to its significant literature, its major strength being its poetry and song. In prose the folk tale was the major genre until modern times when the short story was developed to a highly sophisticated level.

Gaelic poetry from the thirteenth century was practised by professional poets, the most distinguished being the long line of the MacMhuirich bards. They wrote in a classical language which was common to both Scotland and Ireland, and the subjects of their work were such things as panegyrics on their chiefs, clan propaganda and incitements to battle. By the seventeenth century, however, a vernacular tradition which was soon to eclipse the classical bardic tradition had been firmly established. Its first outstanding practitioners were Mairi Nighean Alasdair Ruadh (Mary MacLeod), who wrote fine panegyrics of, among others, the MacLeods of Dunvegan, and Iain Lom (John MacDonald) of Keppoch, a supporter of Montrose, who wrote biting witty political satire.

The eighteenth century, however, witnessed the full flowering of the vernacular tradition with the emergence of such accomplished writers as: Alasdair MacMhaighstir Alasdair (Alexander MacDonald), active supporter of Charles Edward Stuart at the '45, an innovative and accomplished nature poet and a writer of vigorous incitements to battle; Donnachadh Ban nan Oran (Duncan MacIntyre), a keeper from Glen Orchy whose major work 'The Praise of Ben Doran' is a brilliant evocation of nature and deer; and Uilleam Ros (William Ross), a love poet whose 'Oran Eile' is of the highest order. The social turmoil of the Clearances and subsequent land troubles are reflected in the poetry of the nineteenth century, one of the finest practitioners being the Skye poet Mairi Mhòr nan Oran (Mary MacPherson).

In many ways, however, it is the poetry of the twentieth century from the 1930s onward which represents Gaelic poetry's greatest achievement. With the publication of his 'Songs to Eimhir', as Hugh MacDiarmid had done with his 'A Drunk Man Looks at the Thistle', Somhairle MacGilleathain (Sorley MacLean) brought to Gaelic a powerful intellectual modernism incorporating the traditions of the past purged of their sentimentality. He was followed by the equally accomplished modernists, Deorsa Caimbeul Hay (George Campbell Hay), Ruaraidh MacThomais (Derick Thomsom), Iain Mac a'Ghobhainn (Iain Crichton Smith) and Domhnall MacAmhlaigh (Donald MacAulay). The current generation continues strongly with such gifted poets as Aonghas MacNeacail (Angus MacNicol), Mailios Caimbeul (Myles Campbell), Fearghas MacFhionnlaigh (Fergus MacKinlay) and Crisdean Whyte (Christopher Whyte), and, significantly, on the female side with Meg Bateman, Anne Frater and Mairi and Catriona NicGumaraid (Mary and Catriona Montgomery).

As mentioned above, the short story has become a very significant genre in Gaelic writing. Early short stories were very much influenced by the folk tale, but from the 1950s they have become much more taut and sophisticated. Distinguished writers in this field are Pol MacAonghais (Paul MacInnes), Cailein MacCoinnich (Colin MacKenzie), Iain Moireach (John Murray) and, perhaps above all, Iain Mac a'Ghobhainn (Iain Crichton Smith), who has also written the finest Gaelic novel so far, *An t-Aonaran (The Hermit)*.

How are we to give our pupils access to this important strand of their heritage if they have no Gaelic? Obviously there is no substitute for knowing the language itself, but the following approaches may go some way to bridging the gap and hopefully stimulate interest in learning some Gaelic.

PLACE NAMES

The extent of the Gaelic-speaking area over the centuries can be seen from the location of place names which contain Gaelic elements. Furthermore, simply to have some idea of what these names mean is rewarding in itself.

Place names contain two elements, a generic element and a qualifying element. The most common Gaelic generic elements are: inver (river mouth), kin (head), kil (church), bal (village), ach or auch (field). To one of these is added a qualifying element and the name is complete. So 'Kil-bride' means 'the Church of St Bride', 'Inver-aray' means 'the mouth of the river Aray', 'Kin-loch' means 'the head of the loch', etc.

Indeed, if a little time is taken to learn a few generic elements from P-Celtic, Norse and Old English, it will be possible to do a fairly sophisticated analysis of the range of Scottish place names.

POETRY IN TRANSLATION

The most obvious way into Gaelic poetry is through translation and there are many good poetic translations of modern poetry, often by the poets themselves. Some themes which may be particularly rewarding are:

> *War:*   Sorley MacLean – 'Death Valley', 'Going Westward', 'Heroes'.
> George Campbell Hay – 'Bizerta'.

Iain Crichton Smith – 'Going Home'.
Donald MacDonald of North Uist – 'An Eala Bhan' ('The Fair Swan'), sung by Capercaillie on *Cascade*.

Love: William Ross – 'Another Song'.
Sorley MacLean – 'The Choice', 'Dawn', 'Under Sail'.
Angus MacNicol – 'Love Song/Waulking Song', Poem / Fate.
Meg Bateman – 'Because I was so fond of him'.

Nature: Duncan MacIntyre – 'The Praise of Ben Doran' (translated by I. C. Smith).
George Campbell Hay – 'The Smirry Drizzle of Mist'.

Identity: Derick Thomson – 'Coffins', 'I got the feel of you with my feet', 'Sheep'.

Exile: Anon. – 'Sleep softly' (Dean Cadalan Samhach), sung by Capercaillie.
Iain Crichton Smith – 'The Exiles'.

TOPICS

Another way of bridging the gap is to select for study a novel which deals with the Gaelic world in an authentic manner and perhaps enlarge the study of its theme with supplementary Gaelic poems and songs and other texts.

The Montrose Wars: John Splendid (Neil Munro), with Iain Lom's song, 'The Battle of Inverlochy'.

The Jacobite Risings: The New Road (Neil Munro).
The Bull Calves (Naomi Mitchison).
The Flight of the Heron (D. K. Broster).
The Gleam in the North (D. K. Broster).
The Dark Mile (D. K. Broster).
'Young Pennymore', short story by Neil Munro – with such songs as 'Another Song to the Prince' (Alexander MacDonald), 'The Lament for William Chisholm' (Anon.) sung by Capercaillie, 'Culloden Day' (John Roy Stewart).
Campbell of Kilmohr (one-act play by John Brandane).

The Highland *Clearances:*	*Butcher's Broom* (Neil Gunn). *And the Cock Crew* (Fionn MacColla). *Consider the Lilies* (Iain Crichton Smith), with the poem 'Strathnaver' (Derick Thomson). *The Silver Darlings* (Neil Gunn).
Land agitation of *the later nineteenth* *century:*	*Ribbon of Fire* (Alan Campbell MacLean) – for younger readers. *The Lost Glen* (Neil Gunn) – with the songs of Mary MacPherson and Runrig's 'A Dance Called America'. *The Cheviot, the Stag and the Black, Black Oil* (play by John McGrath).
The modern period:	Short stories 'The Telegram' and 'The Wedding' (Iain Crichton Smith). *The Last Summer* (Iain Crichton Smith) with songs by Runrig, e.g. 'O cho meallt'. *The Hill of the Red Fox* (Alan Campbell MacLean) – for younger readers.

BIBLIOGRAPHY

Anthologies

Twentieth century:

Nua-Bhardachd Ghaidhlig (*Modern Scottish Gaelic Poems*), ed. D. MacAulay
    (Edinburgh: Canongate Classics, No. 55, 1995).
An aghaidh na Siorraidheachd (*In the Face of Eternity*), ed. C. Whyte
    (Edinburgh: Polygon, 1991).

Nineteenth century:

Tuath is Tighearna (*Tenants and Landlords*), ed. D. Meek (Edinburgh:
    Scottish Gaelic Texts Society, 1995).

Eighteenth century:

Gaelic Poetry in the Eighteenth Century, ed. D. Thomson (Aberdeen:
    Association for Scottish Literary Studies, 1993).
Highland Songs of the '45, ed. J. L. Campbell (Edinburgh: Scottish Gaelic
    Texts Society, 1984).

Seventeenth century:

Gair nan Clarsach: The Harps' Cry, ed. Colm Ó Baoill and Meg Bateman (Edinburgh: Birlinn, 1994).

Folk tales

Popular Tales of the West Highlands, Vols 1 and 2, ed. J. F. Campbell (Edinburgh: Birlinn, 1994).
Stories from South Uist, Angus MacLellan (London: Routledge & Kegan Paul 1961).

General

A Dictionary of Scottish Place Names, M. Darton (Moffat: Lochar Publications, 1990).
Scotland's Place Names, D. Dorward (Edinburgh: Mercat Press, 1996).
Gaelic Poetry, D. Thomson (London: Gollancz, 1974).
Why Gaelic Matters, D. Thomson (Edinburgh: Saltire Society, 1984).
Gaelic Learner's Handbook, R. MacThòmais, (Glasgow: Gairm Publications).
Companion to Gaelic Scotland, D. S. Thomson (Oxford: Blackwell, 1983).
Gaelic–English Dictionary, E. Dwelly, (Glasgow: Gairm Publications, 1977).
The New English–Gaelic Dictionary, D. S. Thomson (Glasgow: Gairm Publications, 1986).
Gaelic – A Past and Future Prospect, K. Mackinnon, (Edinburgh: Saltire Society, 1991).
Gaelic: Complete Course for Learners, Teach Yourself Books, B. Robertson and I. Taylor (London: Hodder, 1993).

Audio tapes and records

Heartland, Runrig, Ridge Records, 1985).
The Blood is Strong, Capercaillie, Grampian Television Music, 1988.
Catherine-Ann MacPhee Sings Mairi Mhor, Greentrax Recordings, 1994.
14 Poems of Sorley MacLean, ASLS Commentaries, Association for Scottish Literary Studies, 1986.

EXEMPLAR 14

Level/stage of school

S1 to S4 as desired.

Duration

1 or 2 periods.

Topic/texts

A study of local place names, focusing on the languages of origin.

Purposes

> To make the pupils aware of the local and historical significance of the different languages of Scotland.

> To demonstrate the meaningfulness of place names in a particular locality.

Teaching approaches

1. Discuss generally the kinds of place name found in the area of the school. Supply groups of pupils with maps of a section of their own locality; pupils list the main names to be found on the map and try to group them by their apparent linguistic origins (Scots, English, Gaelic, doubtful). Let pupils try this on their own without help.

2. Supply some basic place name elements as a help to pupils in refining their groupings; give access to dictionaries for pupils to do research into the meanings of certain names. Discuss generally the representation of different languages in the local place names, with suggested reasons for any variety.

3. If time permits, try the same exercise with maps of a different locality and observe any obvious variations.

Products

> Classified lists of local place names with the meanings of some.

> Glossaries of basic place name elements and their meanings.

Supporting Materials

A good English dictionary, *Concise Scots Dictionary*, some copies of the *Pocket Scots Dictionary*, a Gaelic dictionary (Dwelly, MacLennan, etc.).

Copies of local maps.

A book like *Scottish Placenames* by W. F. H. Nicolaisen or *Scotland's Place Names* by D. Dorward will be useful for background.

There are also many local publications about place names to be found.

Other comments

Good follow-up writing can be stimulated by reading prose extracts that make use of place names for atmospheric effect. The ways in which names can give colour to writing is a useful study in the development of writing. An interesting poem on this theme is 'American Names' by Stephen Vincent Benet (*Penguin Book of Modern American Verse* or other anthologies), which deals with the effects of place names on the emotions and imagination.

EXEMPLAR 15

Level/stage

S4/5.

Duration

2/3 periods.

Topic/text(s)

Gaelic language and music.
'The Lost Pibroch', story by Neil Munro, and recordings of traditional and modern Gaelic music.
A Para Handy story of the teacher's own choice.

Purposes

To give pupils some awareness of the nature of the Gaelic language and the variety of Gaelic music and song.

To introduce pupils to the writing of a significant Highland writer.

Teaching approaches

1. Supply pupils with copies of the story and accompanying notes and glossary. Read the story, pausing for comment and discussion of the story at appropriate points. Suitable sections are: the opening of the story introducing the theme and the township of Half Town; the arrival of the two pipers in Half Town and their meeting with the blind piper Paruig Dall; the first round of piping; the pipers' conversation about the Lost Pibroch; the playing of the Lost Pibroch; the aftermath and ending.

2. Discuss with pupils how Munro has conveyed the atmosphere and traditions of the old Highlands, using language and reference. How does the idea of the Lost Pibroch and its effects have a connection with the real decline and death of the traditional Highland way of life?

3. Move on to the idea of Gaelic music. Discuss a number of examples of music played on tape: pipe music, including pibroch; traditional songs; dance music; modern rock music derived from the Gaelic tradition. Why has this kind of music, originating in one part of Scotland, come to be regarded as typical of Scotland as a whole?

4. Refer to Neil Munro's other writing, especially the Para Handy stories. Read one of the Para Handy stories and discuss what has happened to the image of the Highlander in this story.

Products

Pupils' notes on the stories and the music.

Supporting materials

Taped recordings of Gaelic music and song, including Runrig and Capercaillie.

A Gaelic dictionary as desired.

Other comments

This work can be used as an introduction to the writing of Neil Munro as a possible Review of Personal Reading topic. The other short stories in *The Lost Pibroch* can be read separately as desired. They would generally work at the Standard Grade level.

EXEMPLAR 16

Level/stage of school

S4.

Duration

2 periods.

Topic/text(s)

'Coffins' ('Cisteachan-Laighe') by Derick Thomson: study of poem dealing with the loss of Gaelic culture and language.

Purposes

To help the class to an awareness of the way in which a culture and language may be weakened to the point of death over a couple of generations by social and educational attitudes.

To introduce pupils to the work of a major contemporary Gaelic poet.

Teaching approaches

1. Read the English version of the poem with the class. If possible, let them hear a reading of it in Gaelic. Discuss the situation of the poem: memories of the grandfather and his occupation as joiner and coffin-maker; memory of his funeral when the poet was a boy; the boy's lack of awareness of how his education was turning him into a coffin, killing the living culture and language that he carried inside him; awareness of the process when it was too late.

2. Wider discussion of how true this is of people growing up in a society that does not value their home and family traditions. Discuss the relevance to Gaelic today, with social and popular attitudes to Gaelic. Apply also to Scots language and culture, and pupils' feelings about the language and culture of their grandparents; discuss also any other cultures and languages relevant to pupils in the class or that they know of from their experience or reading.

3. Discuss whether this is in fact the experience of the poet or if he is describing a process that he has managed to avoid, being obviously a

Gaelic scholar himself.

4. Possible creative or discursive writing can follow up the discussions. A story or poem, or an essay, drawing on other kinds of experience to comment on how education is used to shape and mould people into a socially or politically desired product.

Products

Pupils' writings.

Supporting materials

Tape of Gaelic reading of poem.

Other materials (newspaper articles, photographs, etc.) on Gaelic culture.

Other comments

This can be an introduction to Derick Thomson's poetry. Other poems worth reading include: 'The Herring Girls', 'Sheep', 'The Scarecrow', 'The Well', etc.

EXEMPLAR 17

Level/stage of school

S3/4.

Duration

2 periods.

Topic/text(s)

Short story: 'The Wedding' by Iain Crichton Smith.

Purposes

To make pupils aware of some of the factors affecting the loss of Gaelic culture and tradition.

To study one of the works of a major contemporary Scottish novelist and poet.

Teaching approaches

1. Read the story with the class, pausing where appropriate to discuss the progress of the story. A suitable way of breaking up the story would be to take the natural stages of the occasion: outside the church; the wedding ceremony and photographs; the arrival at the reception and the meal; the speeches; the dancing and singing afterwards.

2. Discuss different aspects of the story, possibly in groups. (*A Third Book of Modern Scottish Stories* has some helpful commentary and talking points.) Likely aspects to focus on are: the attitude of the narrator to the occasion; the younger guests and their attitudes; the bride and groom; the parents of the bride, especially the father; the differences between the father's generation and the bride's; the father's way of life and cultural tradition. A possible talking point to introduce is a traditional Gaelic song played on tape set against some typical wedding dance music.

3. The differences between the two generations seem to belong to a period that is now past, the 1950s and 1960s. How different would the wedding be today? Can any of the pupils bring their own experiences at family weddings to the discussion? What factors were affecting the situation in the story, and are they still affecting occasions of this sort? What is the apparent view of the *author*, which is not necessarily that of the narrator in the story?

4. Possible follow-up writing might be about a similar family occasion, as observed by the pupils, with some reflection on how the older and younger generations have different preferences and attitudes.

Products

Pupils' notes on the story.

Pupils' writing as follow-up.

Supporting materials

Copies of story.

Help sheets with talking points for group discussion.

Taped recording of Gaelic song and popular dance music.

Other comments

This story would be a good accompaniment to the study of the poetry of Derick Thomson, especially 'Coffins'.

EXEMPLAR 18

Level/stage of school

S3/4.

Duration

1/2 periods.

Topic/text(s)

An examination of racial prejudice: 'How the First Hielandman Was Made' (Anon.).

Purposes

To read an Older Scots text, noting its language features, its humour and its narrative skill.

To discuss the topic of racial and other prejudice, firstly as shown in this text directed against Gaelic Highlanders, secondly as shown in modern Scotland against not only Highlanders but also other groups within Scottish society.

Teaching approaches

1. The text of the poem is supplied to pupils and read together. There is then discussion of points from the poem, notably the language, the humour, the vivid dramatic down-to-earth treatment of God, St Peter and the Highlandman.

2. The prejudice shown against the Highlander can be discussed by pupils in groups, followed by discussion of targets of prejudice in contemporary Scotland. Is prejudice made more 'acceptable' by being humorous? Can stories at the expense of an identifiable group of people within society be

excused, or is it an inescapable element of humour?

3. Some discursive writing on the subject might be a suitable way of rounding off the topic, perhaps a criticism of the anonymous writer of the poem.

Products

Pupils' writings.

Annotated copies of the poem.

Supporting materials

Leaflets and other publicity about prejudice.

Another poem or text about prejudice as desired.

Other comments

The longstanding prejudice against the Gael felt by Lowland Scots is a big topic deserving some more detailed treatment. There are many historical examples of this from the Middle Ages right down to modern times, yet it does not surface very often in literature. Neil Gunn's novel *Butcher's Broom* provides some good examples of prejudice used as justification for the harshness of the Clearances.

5

THE SCOTS LANGUAGE IN THE SCHUIL

John Hodgart

Shairly ane o the maist absurd paradoxes o Scottish culture is that oor ain independent educational system has played a major pairt in pitten doon the native tungs o Scotland, baith Scots an Gaelic. Yet while in the Gaelic speakin areas the language has lang syne won its richtfu place in the curriculm, in Lowland Scotland things hae buin gey different. Here, as wi mony aspects o Scottish culture, we are suspendit in a sort o Alice thro the keekin gless world, whaur we hae tae actually justify the teachin o the native language o the country tae oor ain weans. Nae doot monie Scottish teachers react wi predictable scorn at the very idea, while some actually feel threatent bi this suggestion, seein it as 'an imposition' or even worse, some kinna discrimination agin weans that dinnae yaise 'Scots'!

Thus we are still a culturally colonised nation, for tragically the dinnae say 'ay' mentality is still deeply implantit in ower mony Scots' heids, lik a genetic tumour, sae that we are socially condeetiont tae accept that there's only ane 'correct' wey for educatit folk tae speak an write, an it certainly isnae in the native tung. In fact maist Scots dinnae even recognise their ain local vernacular as 'Scots', as they've been led tae believe that it is at best a 'corrupt' dialect o English, an at worst, pure dead common slang, the language o the sheugh. Nae wunner aw the distinctive features o oor speech, whether vocabulary, pronunciation or grammar are maistly seen as jist 'bad' English, insteid o 'guid' Scots: the distinctive features o a kizzen tung that shares common ruits wi English but has develpt in different weys ower the centuries (see the Introduction to the *Concise Scottish Dictionary*).

While we cuid gae roon in circles tryin tae prove that Scots is a 'language', as opposed tae jist a dialect, we hae the linguistic evidence o oor dictionaries that show the range an variety o Scots vocabulary, syntax an grammar are faur mair extensive than onie ither 'dialect' in the English-speakin world, shairly somethin tae be gey prood o, no ashamed o: somethin tae inspire oor weans in the richness an richtness o their ain speech, an tae see it as a leivin an continuin parts o a reuch auld tung.

Yet in spite o aw the educational an social prejudices tryin tae kill aff Lowland Scots, Lallans, the Doric or the Patter (or whitever variety ye mean), it thrawnly refuses tae wither awa, for its ruits are teuch an deep, as maist Scots continue yaisin it in some form, or at least unnerstaun it. For a gey lang while noo, middle-class dominies hae buin claimin that Scots has 'died out', but if they really opens their lugs, they micht weel be surprised tae fin that monie Scots weans still speak some form o Scots, an no jist in rural Scotland. Tho they micht no yaise it tae their teachers, an it micht no aye be thocht o as 'Scots', especially in the central urban areas, the native or 'natural', speech o maist weans still isnae Standard English.

Thus the majority o Scots weans are still faced wi a double linguistic handicap: furstly in learnin that the language they speak ootside or at hame isnae the language spoken in the classroom, an saicontly, tryin tae mak the switch fae the spoken tae the written word, for the language o literacy isnae in their dialect, but a mair formal, mair impersonal an generally mair middle-class dialect. Fae the meenit they enter the classroom, or in some cases the playgroup, they learn that some forms o speech are acceptit, an ithers arenae, a sort o linguistic kincher that they hae tae learn tae unfankle as suin as possible afore educators will actually listen tae whit they're sayin, insteid o how they're sayin it.

Tragically, Scottish education has faur too often crushed Scots weans' confidence in this wey, creatin a painfu crisis o identity an cultural loyalties, an especially for workin class weans, makkin them reject an education system that rejects thaim. Ironically some argue that 'imposin' Scots on weans that naturally speak English 'will result in an inarticulate and tongue-tied people'! Nae doot it's aw richt tae gae on daein the opposite: imposin a policy o linguistic cleansin, tae protect an perpetuate a linguistic status quo that favours middle-class weans. Thus no only hae the policies o the past buin psychologically damagin in contributin tae oor endemic cultural cringe an uncertainties aboot how tae express oorsels, but they hae buin socially divisive in reinforcin the worst aspects o social snobbery an class division: a dangerous an destructive educational approach that shid hae nae place in the educational system o ony modern democratic society.

However, prejudice aginst Scots isnae the same for aw forms o Scots, as opeenions aboot whit in fact qualifies as 'Scots' often causes mony a catterbatter, as some forms o Scots, mainly the aulder rural dialects, lik the Nor East 'Doric', are thocht o as genuine or 'pure', while the mair recent urban dialects are seen as degenerate or slovenly. Thus it is a fairly common assumption amang teachers that some forms o Scottish speech are 'OK', but ithers are jist a mongrel mixture o slangs an patter: for mony o oor urban weans a double barrier o prejudice, in learnin on the ane haun, that they speak 'bad' English, an on the ither haun bein tellt that they speak 'bad' Scots tae. Thus they cannae win, whitever wey they turn, an nae wunner they are often dismisst as inarticulate mummlers bi their middle class teachers. Yet shairly as language teachers we need tae tackle this kinna ignorance, for we hae a duty as educatit folk tae combat aw forms o prejudice, especially aboot how oor weans shid express theirsels.

If we really want tae develop the linguistic confidence o aw oor pupils, Scottish teachers sairly need tae get awa fae this nerra-nebbit notion o whit Scots is or isnae, an stop believin in the auld myth that 'guid' Scots wis whit their grannie spoke, aye in the past, aye somewhaur else, no the actual speech yaised bi their weans in front o them. We need in fact tae accept that the 'best' Scots is whit the local weans bring tae their ain schuil in aw its varieties; tae stert fae whaur the weans are at, linguistically speakin, respect the wey they talk, an build their linguistic development an confidence fae there, insteid o giein them the double penalty o tellin them that they neither speak 'good' English, nor 'guid' Scots.

Anither complication for the linguistic purists is that, as kizzen tungs, Scots an English hae aye owerlapped, wi a relationship that can be described as a linguistic continuum, for they shade intae ane anither, an it isnae aye possible tae say whaur ane sterts an anither feenishes. Indeed the reality o Scottish speech the day is that it is gey inconsistent, or gey fluid, dependin on how ye see it, for maist Scots range across the linguistic spectrum on a mair or less basis, varyin the nummer o distinctive Scots features in oor speech, fae a mair dense local Scots, tae a middle gruin whaur we style shift or drift intae a distinctive form o Scots Standard English.

Hopefully the time has noo arrived that we can see this mixed state o Scots an English no as a problem, but as an opportunity, a bilingual reality that is a source o a unique linguistic flexibility. In fact some o oor maist famous writers o the past valued the positive aspects o bein able tae mix Scots an English, an bein able tae yaise ane whaur the ither wis lackin, fae Henryson an Dunbar at the very hicht o the language's achievement, tae Ramsay, Burns an Galt in the eighteenth and nineteenth centuries, while ane o the maist interestin aspects o contemporary Scots writin is the clever wey the mixed state o Scots an English has buin exploitit, wi aw sorts o skeely contrasts an combinations bein experimentit wi, somethin that widnae be possible if they only wrote in the ane language:

> I would rather see the mixed state that exists being explored and exploited ... It may be that we have a blessing in disguise. But if we want to uncover it we shall have to use our ears more and our grammar books less. (Morgan, 1974)

Thus the reality micht weel be that modern Scots potentially offers a faur mair flexible register than English can, a feature described bi a skeely translator o foreign plays intae Scots, Bill Findlay, as 'a very rich resource, perhaps unique in the English speaking world'. As teachers o language an literature in Scotland, is it really no aboot time that we woke up tae this tremendous linguistic potential inherent in Scottish culture, insteid o continuin tae be obsessed wi 'correctness' an repressive monolingual policies o the past?

Indeed it wid seem that in the last quarter o the twintieth century a lot o folk in the Scottish educational system hae begun tae realise that in bein bilingual, we actually hae a great cultural asset, thro bein able tae express oorsels wi equal confidence in baith Scots an English. Nae greater pruif o a linguistic revolution in official thinkin is the fact that it is noo SED policy tae encourage Scots an Gaelic in oor schuils, fae 5–14 throu tae the new Highers, tho sayin a thing an actually daein it is a different maitter aw thegither, for I doot if maist English teachers, nevermind ithers, hae come tae terms wi the linguistic implications o these policies.

The enthusiastic response o maist o the teachers surveyed for the SCCC project, *The Kist*, is a hertenin sign that monie Scottish teachers will leuk on this duty positively, but nae doot maist teachers an parents will need time tae sclim ower the high wa o their ain language condeetionin. At the same time we really need tae spell oot that if teachers only gie Scottish language an culture an 'odd' period, noo an again (e.g. the annual Burns piece) they are failin in their duties as defined in the *5–14 Guidelines* (SOED, 1991). In effect it really has tae be gien its richtfu place at the very hert o the language programme in primary an saicondary. Yet monie English teachers still see ony challenge tae established monolingual policies as a threat tae oor duties as, literally, teachers o English, an that accomodatin ony kinna Scots is an 'imposition' we coud weel dae withoot!

While *5–14* is in mony weys a maist positive document, wi its comments aboot cultural an linguistic diversity, an the schuil's need tae 'strive to promote the status of all the languages used in the school community in significant ways' (SOED, 1991, p. 59), it's really left up tae the Gaelic Guidelines tae spell oot 'the advantages of bi-lingualism for teaching and learning – not least for the acquisition of yet more languages.' Indeed aw the educational evidence noo pynts tae the fact that bilingual weans are gleg an skeely weans, wi in-built linguistic an creative advantages, nevermind a facility for learnin ither languages, somethin that monolingual policies mak mair diffficult. Therefore while we hae tae sympathise wi teachers' fears, we shairly need tae ask whether a lot o oor deep-ruitit linguistic problems micht no in fact wither awa if we challenged oor monolingual condeetionin (the exception rether than the rule in maist countries, an a relic o imperialism) an, lik plenty o oor European neebours, learnt tae think in terms o bilingualism or bidialectism in oor schuils (for example Catalonia, whaur bilingual policies o cultural 'normalisation' hae buin successfully developt.

Tae reassure parents an employers tho, we'd hae tae spell oot that at the core o such a programme wid remain oor duty tae teach the basic skills o literacy an develop confidence in aw the communication skills. Yet insteid o daein this only via standard English, we wid be aimin tae achieve this bi extendin their linguistic confidence an skills throu explorin the hail range o the native language in its main Scots an English forms, as spellt oot in the HMI Report *Effective Learning and Teaching* (SOED, 1992, p. 6).

Shairly this wid address the linguistic reality o the majority o oor pupils, thereby giein them mair confidence in their ain powers o communication, an help Scottish education tae see Scots an English as complementary tae ane anither. Tae achieve this we'll need furstly tae convince teachers that copin wi some degree o bidialectism isnae mibbie such a big linguistic lowp efter aw, somethin that they need tae be completely retrained tae cope wi, for we can stert bi buildin on the skills o linguistic flexibility that probably maist o us already hae in communicatin wi weans. In fact mibbie we cuid learn mair jist bi listenin better tae some o oor weans, for monie o thaim hae had tae learn some o the skills o bilingualism for theirsels, bi keepin English for the classroom but Scots for friens or hame. An even if they dinnae speak, or dinnae think they speak, some form o Scots, nae maitter hoo sheltert their upbringin, shairly they will someday need tae unnerstaun somebody that actually speaks tae them in Scots?

Therefore, jist as it is vital that talkin an listenin shid involve a mixture o Scots an English in a variety o forms, readin an writin skills shid folla naturally on fae this, for if we only gie oor weans readin material in standard English an ask them tae dae aw their writin in it, we are no only failin tae teach them a sufficient range o linguistic skills an registers, but staun guilty o linguistic neglect bi makkin Scots weans illiterate in their native culture. Thus it isnae enough tae say that since our children don't speak Scots it is pointless teaching them to be literate in it, for if the language programmes in Scottish schuils can be democratised throu a policy o linguistic tolerance, diversity an flexibility, oor weans will learn faur mair aboot the nature o language an languages than fae a conventional monolingual education. At the same time they will hopefully develop a faur mair flexible range, freshness an originality o expression than the 'correct' but often lifeless standard English that maist weans think they 'huvtae' yaise aw the time, even in 'creative' writin.

In some weys we cuid see Scottish literature an language as an Equal Opportunities issue: askin for the same democratic richts for aw dialect speakers that only speakers o the standard variety hae enjoyed up tae noo. Abuin aw, Scots has a richtfu place in oor schuils in terms o respectin oor ain cultural identity, an identity that is linguistically complex an diverse, an we need tae see this diversity as an inherent cultural strength, no a weakness.

If we can see oor identity in terms o concentric circles o linguistic an cultural relationships, mibbie we will stert tae appreciate the strengths we hae in oor midst, tae accept that ane circle disnae cancel oot the ither, but exists within, an reinforces the ither, but at the core lies a centre we hae confidence in. This willnae be the same core for awbody, for we hae many different 'mither' tungs in oor midst, tho mony o them are gey closely interconnectit. Scotland has aye buin a multiracial an multilingual culture, an we noo need tae come tae terms wi this in oor educational system an in the media. If we really are serious aboot defendin oor diverse cultural identity, an mibbie tryin tae cure oor perverse cultural cringe, we need tae mak siccar that aw weans lea the schuil literate in the native tungs o Scotland as weel as oor ain distinctive form o standard English.

Thus we micht hae a really Scottish educational system tae be prood o, ane that wid value an develop the rich linguistic heritage o a Scotland o mony different tungs, includin the new anes brocht here bi mair recent incomers. If ither wee countries, or minority cultures can manage this, why no us? For if oor ain Scottish educational system cannae learn how tae cope wi educatin oor weans in the native languages, sae that Scots an English complement ane anither, Scottish teachers will continue tae dae whit they hae duin ower lang – betray Scottish culture.

BIBLIOGRAPHY

Aitken, A. J. and T. McArthur (eds), *The Languages of Scotland* (London: Chambers, 1979).

Kay, W., *The Mither Tongue* (Edinburgh: Mainstream, 1986, 1993).

McClure, J. D., *Why Scots Matters* (Edinburgh: Saltire Society, 1988).

McClure, J. D. (ed.) *Scotland and the Lowland Scots Tongue* (Aberdeen: Aberdeen University Press, 1983).

Morgan, E. (1974) 'Registering the Reality of Scotland', in *Essays* (Cheadle: Carcanet, 1974).

Murison, D., *The Guid Scots Tongue* (Edinburgh: Blackwood, 1977).

SOED, *National Guidelines: English Language 5–14* (Edinburgh: SOED, 1991).

SOED, *Effective Learning and Teaching in Scottish Secondary Schools: English*, HMI Report (Edinburgh: SOED, 1992).

SOED, *Provision for Gaelic Education in Scotland*, HMI Report (Edinburgh: SOED, 1994).

Trudgill, P., *Accent, Dialect and the School* (London: Arnold, 1975).

EXEMPLAR 19

Level/stage of school

S1/2.

Duration

As required.

Topic/text(s)

The variety of forms of Scots language through time and place. *The Kist/A' Chiste* and other teacher-chosen texts in varieties of Scots.

Purposes

> To make pupils aware of how Scots language varies within Scotland now and has changed from past to present.

> To encourage pupils to read and enjoy Scots writing of different styles and forms.

Teaching approaches

1. Read aloud to the class or let them listen to recordings of four pieces of Scots writing: one modern (from anywhere in Scotland), one antique, one in urban dialect, one in rural dialect. After each, discuss with the class what they can decide about the origin of each from the language and from context.

2. Provide groups with copies of *The Kist*, plus a number of other Scots pieces of different types (including a number of Older Scots pieces, e.g. from the *Penguin* or *Oxford Book of Scottish Verse*). Ask groups to read and choose about six texts for including in a class anthology of Scots writing. They should try and label each as either old or modern, and indicate which district or city of Scotland it comes from.

3. Once the groups have completed their task, the group choices should be discussed and definite conclusions reached about where each piece has come from, before they are arranged and collected into a class anthology.

4. An extension of the work is to have pupils write their own pieces (verse or prose) in their own natural language (which may not be Scots) for inclusion in the anthology. The final collection can be copied, bound and illustrated as desired. Groups might write possible introductions to the anthology to give information about it to possible readers.

Products

A class Scots anthology.

Individual pupil writings.

Supporting materials

Teacher's selection of Scots texts to add to *The Kist*.

Scots School Dictionary, and other Scots word books as available.

A map of Scotland to check localities.

Other comments

This is only one of a number of ways to make pupils aware of the variety of the Scots language. At some point in the language syllabus, there should be a more structured study of the historical development and geographical distribution of the Scots language.

EXEMPLAR 20

Level/stage of school

S1–3 (as desired).

Duration

1 or 2 periods.

Topic/Text

'Call My Bluff': Scots language game.

Purposes

To explore, have fun with and learn about Scots vocabulary.

Teaching approaches

1. Divide class into teams of three pupils each; each team prepares plausible definitions (one true, two false) for two chosen obscure Scots words.

2. Two teams play each other, with teacher or a pupil as chairperson and scorer, presenting their words in turn for the other team to guess; the process is repeated with two fresh teams, and repeated until all teams have played. If there is time, winning teams can play each other with new words until there is one overall winning team.

3. Words and correct definitions can be displayed on wall in a growing visual dictionary. Other words encountered in the course of work on Scots language can be added as well.

Products

Wall dictionary display.

Pupils' Scots word books.

Pupils' writing using some of the words.

Supporting materials

The Scots Thesaurus – an invaluable source of Scots words arranged by topics.

The Concise Scots Dictionary.

Other comments

Word games with Scots words are a valuable and enjoyable way to bring such words to pupils' attention, probably as a preliminary to encouraging their use in pupils' writing. Scrabble and Countdown are other obvious games for this treatment, but pupils have to generate the words themselves, which will not produce a very original selection at first. However, if the games are played regularly, then pupils' own vocabularies will grow.

EXEMPLAR 21

Level/stage of school

S1/2.

Duration

As required.

Topic/text(s)

Study of Scots words on particular themes, using *The Scots Thesaurus*.

Purposes

To widen pupils' knowledge of Scots words.

To give pupils practice in using Scots words in appropriate contexts.

Teaching approaches

1. Copy sections from *The Scots Thesaurus* on weather, and make up five or six sets for groups. Make a similar number of sets of selected Scots

weather words (without meanings given) for discussion.

2. Discuss weather with pupils, referring to TV weather forecasts. Distribute sets of Scots weather words to groups. Pupils discuss them and ascribe meanings to them. Further discussion of pupils' suggested meanings before checking with thesaurus sets.

3. Pupils make collages of weather pictures (from magazine illustrations) with Scots words added as captions.

4. To complete work, each group prepares a Scots weather forecast for taping (with charts if video is used).

Products

Illustrations of Scots weather terms.

Taped Scots weather forecasts.

Supporting materials

The Scots Thesaurus.

Copies of the *Pocket Scots Dictionary* as desired.

Magazines/supplements as sources for pictures.

Other comments

The same process can be applied to topics like food and drink (with menus and recipes), personal characteristics (with descriptions, 'Wanted' posters), animals and birds, etc.

EXEMPLAR 22

Level/stage of school

S4/5.

Duration

3 periods.

Topic/text(s)

Bilingualism in society: poem, 'This is thi six a clock news' by Tom Leonard.

Purposes

To introduce pupils to the concept of bilingualism.

To examine attitudes to the use of Scots (or Gaelic) in different situations.

To encourage and practise the speaking and writing of Scots in an 'official' situation.

Teaching approaches

1. Read the Tom Leonard poem and discuss the attitudes to Scots and English that it satirises, including the notion that one kind of language is suitable for an official function like reading the national news while another is not.

2. Listen to a number of recorded news summaries from different radio channels (Radio 1, 2, Scotland, Classic FM, Clyde, etc.) and discuss the attitudes to the news and the listeners that they suggest.

3. In groups, have pupils work on writing news items (taken from recordings and from newspapers) in Scots (or Gaelic or any other language belonging to pupils).

4. Build up group news bulletins of several items in Scots and other languages, and record readings.

5. Discuss whether it is better to have official media broadcasting in any one language (a standard) or in a variety of languages reflecting the consumers' languages, i.e. to promote a monolingual or a bilingual (or multilingual) policy for authoritative social purposes. Consider what other kinds of social situations might be regarded as suitable for bilingual expression.

Products

Recorded news bulletins from groups.

Supporting materials

Recordings of radio news summaries.

Newspapers as sources of news items.

Copies of *The Scots School Dictionary*.

Other comments

Some pupils might have experience of other countries or societies where there is a bilingual (or multilingual) policy. Teachers could find out what happens in some other countries of Europe where there is more than one national or community language.

6

———— • ————

LEARNING ME MY LANGUAGE

Morna R. Fleming

Whenever two or three Scots are gathered together for a literary discussion, sooner or later 'the language thing' will arise and a more or less violent argument ensue. Periodically in the letters page of *The Scotsman* or *The Herald* there is a similar flyting, and whenever there is a revision of the school English (sic) curriculum, the question of the place of Scottish language and literature will arise. A glance at *Scottish Literature in the Secondary School*, a report on a subcommittee on the study of Scottish Literature in schools (HMSO, 1976), *Guidelines on English Language 5–14* (SOED, 1991) and *Developing Scottish Literature* (SCCC, 1990) will show that the same debate has been continuing for the past 20 years, and there is little prospect of its being resolved in the foreseeable future. The root cause of the debate is the language itself, and the status of the Scots language in Scotland today, but even that apparently simple issue is fraught with ambiguity.

What *is* Scots, after all? Scots is the language spoken by Scottish people in Scotland, whatever their origins.[1] It covers a spectrum from the broadest Doric of the north-east or the dialect of Shetland to the most 'polite' Morningside or Kelvinside English, and excludes virtually no form of expression. As William Neill describes it, 'the leid of the skuil wes Scottish Stannart Inglish ...; the leid o maist ither fowk (in the Auld Toun) wes Scots o varyin depth an lexis.'[2] Given such a wide definition, it is perhaps easier to specify what is *not* Scots, namely the language of what A. J. Aitken calls 'the laird class', the 'high status accent of English origin which is obligatory in "county" circles in both England and Scotland.'[3] Importantly, from my point of view, Scots includes the way I speak and write.

Although I speak that version of Scots known as Scottish Standard English, I am aware of Scots idiomatic usages which are foreign to me. I should never refer to 'the man that ...', as 'the man who ...' is more natural, nor should I ask someone where he 'stays', as my idiom would be 'lives'. I am aware of Scots alternatives for vocabulary items: I know the words and understand them when I hear them spoken, and I can deliberately use a Scots word for effect, very much in the same way that one might use a French or German word in an English sentence, but, apart from 'pinkie' for the little finger, 'rones' for roof gutters, 'bramble' for blackberry and 'wee' for small, I would never use them in everyday language.

My natural idiom in spoken as in written language is part of my cultural identity. This is obviously accounted for by my upbringing in Edinburgh and latterly in Dundee, although my parents came originally from Fife, as did my maternal grandparents. Despite what I now know to be the rich linguistic heritage of the fishing villages in the Kingdom, I was familiar as a child only with the Standard Scottish English spoken within the family. True, my grandmother did always serve meat, often a 'gigot' of lamb, on an 'ashet', but the only true Older Scots expressions I was ever aware of were when, on one of our frequent outings in the car, Grandad would tell us that it would not matter if we got lost, because he could 'speir', and if we were misbehaving, he would threaten to 'sort' us.

This does not mean to say that I devalue or disparage Scots language and literature. Neither do I feel that I can only teach Scots literature written in Scottish Standard English. Since studying for an MPhil. in Scottish Literature, I have taken a great number of Scots texts from the earliest times right up to the present into the classroom, and have encouraged the rest of my department to use such texts as widely as possible with all age groups and abilities. In some areas of fairly predictable study, such as poetry of the First World War, I have found refreshingly new viewpoints from Scottish writers to put alongside or (even) to substitute for those of Owen and Sassoon.

Bringing more Scottish texts into the classroom and encouraging pupils in the Fife school that I teach in to explore their own language resources has taught me more about contemporary Fife Scots and I have, I hope, given pupils an interest in the variations in language. It has certainly shown me that there is still infinite variety, as even within a small county like Fife there are vocabulary items and some idiomatic usages which are peculiar to a very small area, the differences having arisen from the predominant occupation of the region, whether fishing, farming or coal-mining.

However, although they are recognised Scots speakers, when I present the Scots of Burns, Soutar, Garioch, Jacob or MacDiarmid, never mind that of Dunbar, Henryson or Barbour, to my pupils it is initially met with utter blankness and little comprehension. What is needed is a bridge from the language of the past, or from one idiom to another, by means of carefully chosen texts whose subject matter pupils can relate to and discuss in their own terms. This is not at all difficult to achieve, when one considers that Scots writers have always been interested in people and their lives: growing up, relationships, fears, the realities of living and the sometimes supernatural possibilities of the imagination. Even the physical process of delivering these texts to pupils need not be a daunting prospect when one considers the considerable range of taped material where texts are given the most authentic reading possible.[4] It would, I think, be preferable, however, if the teacher were, after some practice, to attempt to read him or herself, as otherwise there could be a perception of alienation.

We do not want Scottish children to think of Scots as a foreign language, rather one that they are unfamiliar with but can learn to enjoy as they can learn to enjoy the 'difficult' English of Shakespeare or Eliot or Hopkins. This can be achieved by reading and talking (in their own terms) about the texts. No one should advocate that pupils be asked to write in this new form, unless, of course, they are themselves inspired to do so, and exposure to the writing of James Kelman, Irvine Welsh, Iain Banks, Janice Galloway, A. L. Kennedy and others who have so recently found favour with the London literati will show them that their own contemporary language is both capable of expressing literary opinions and of producing the literature on which such opinion is formed.

Contemporary writing in Scotland, as might be expected, exemplifies the debate. A trawl through recent issues of *New Writing Scotland* shows a vibrancy of language and an acknowledgement of the whole spectrum of Scots, including the prose Doric of Ronald McDonald and John Aberdein. As a reflection of the current linguistic situation in Scotland, there is a vast preponderance of Scottish Standard English pieces, prose and poetry, with more Gaelic than Burnsian Scots in most issues, apart from in some of the poetry. Editors throughout the 1990s have consistently mentioned the linguistic diversity in the submissions received, which, according to editorial policy, are invited in 'any of the languages of Scotland'. Janice Galloway and Hamish Whyte, 1992 editors of NWS issue 10, entitled *Pig Squealing*, specifically mention their approval of the refusal 'to deal with the inverted commas kind of "Scottishness" and instead examine the old questions in a new way'.[5]

What exemplifies the vitality of Scottish culture, as represented in *New Writing Scotland*, regardless of the language in which it is expressed, is the number of unforced allusions to European culture and literature, showing the outgoing attitude and willingness to sample all that is best in a variety of cultures that has always characterised the literate Scot. Translations into Scots of French classics from Molière and Rostand[6] are part of a continuum from the Renaissance in the time of James VI and provide an alternative to the English translation. We have always been outgoers, explorers, snappers up of unconsidered trifles from the languages of every invader or ally we have dealt with, many of whom have left their distinguishing marks on place names and geographical features, the common starting point for language study in primary schools, to enrich children's understanding of their heritage and of differences between cultures even within one country.

Until fairly recent times there has been a feeling in some quarters that writing in anything other than Standard English was in some way 'unacceptable', and had to be accounted for by the social class or geographical origins of the character concerned. It is up to teachers like me, native Scottish Standard English speakers, to introduce much more Scottish literature from all ages and in all languages into classrooms, so that, as David Purves puts it, 'children will understand that certain features of their natural speech are not due to the ignorance of their parents, but are the remnants of what was once a fine garment – a national language with an unrestricted range of expression.'[7]

NOTES

1. Prof. Magnus Fladmark in the Report of the SATE Conference on 25 February 1995 estimates that 80 per cent of households speak Scots. See *The Speak*, October 1995, p. 5.
2. William Neill (1985) 'The Ruit an the Flooer', *Chapman*, Vol. 41, p. 24.
3. *Scottish Literature in the Secondary School* (HMSO, 1976), p. 50.
4. Taped materials are produced by ASLS, Scotsoun, BBC, School of Scottish Studies, etc.
5. Introduction to *Pig Squealing*, issue 10 of *New Writing Scotland* published by ASLS (1992).
6. Such as those by Liz Lochhead and Edwin Morgan.
7. David Purves (1985) 'The Present State of Scots', *Chapman*, Vol. 41, p. 33.

EXEMPLAR 23

Level/stage of school

S4/5.

Duration

2+ periods.

Topic/text(s)

Classical allusion in literature, using the story of Sisyphus as an example: poem 'Sisyphus' by Robert Garioch; extract from *The Bridge* by Iain Banks (the descent of the Glasgow Barbarian to Hades).

Purposes

To introduce pupils to two very different kinds of Scots language in modern literature.

To show how a modern writer may use a classical story or myth for comic or other effect.

Teaching approaches

1. Provide copies of the texts, the poem being distributed first. Read the poem aloud more than once to help understanding of the difficult Scots vocabulary through sound associations and context clues. Use dictionaries for any obstinate textual problems. Discuss how the poem is both funny in itself and serious in its application to modern work and people's attitudes to it.

2. Compare the Garioch version with a standard account of the classical story of Sisyphus as found in a collection of the Greek myths. Move on to remind pupils of other features of Greek mythology and inmates of Hades: the River Lethe, Charon the boatman, Cerberus, Tantalus, Prometheus, Medusa the Gorgon, etc.

3. Provide copies of the Iain Banks extract for pupils to read themselves in groups and discuss to work out meaning. The problems of unacceptable language can be dealt with as the teacher wishes, but most pupils will be quite undisturbed. Topics for discussion can include the nature of the Barbarian's language, the humour of the Glasgow sensibility meeting the classical figures and upsetting the well-established mythological routines, etc. Some pupils will be aware of the Swords and Sorcery fantasy genre in books and films (e.g. Conan the Barbarian) which will be a useful comparison. References within the extract to the wider plot of *The Bridge* can safely be ignored.

4. The topic can be concluded with a comparison of the two texts in terms of language, discussing how they represent perhaps two different attitudes to the use of Scots language in literature, the restoration of older Scots forms and the use of popular speech forms.

Products

Pupil notes on language and myths.

Supporting materials

Concise Scots Dictionary.

Other comments

Further work can continue into a study of other Garioch poems, especially his sonnets, or into RPR work on Iain Banks novels.

EXEMPLAR 24

Level/stage of school

S1/2.

Duration

I week of class time.

Topic/text(s)

'The Taill of the Uponlandis Mous and the Burges Mous' (Robert Henryson), in a simplified and glossed version, as in the *Oxford Book of Scottish Verse*: perhaps part of a study of fables and legends.

Purposes

To introduce younger pupils to Older Scots in a manageable and entertaining form, using a story that they will probably already be familiar with.

To make pupils aware of the idea of learning through a reading of didactic literature which draws moral lessons from a story.

Teaching approaches

1 Pupils, under the guidance of the teacher, collectively reconstruct and retell the story of the Town Mouse and the Country Mouse.

2. The version of the story by Aesop is read by the class, if it is available, to show how bald and undeveloped it is.

3. The Henryson fable is read by the teacher or heard on tape (preferably in sections, interspersed with clarifying discussion and commentary). Once it is established and fully understood, the different scenes of the poem are worked out and each group takes a scene to work on (about five or six stanzas per group.

4. Each group illustrates their scene, using cut-out pictures from magazines, Clip-Art, lettering or calligraphy pattern books, and their own drawing to convey a strong visual impression of the scene. Illuminated lettering and pictures and cartoon images will build up a collage. Alternatively, a more unified storyboard can be produced.

5. Finally, the class will discuss how to present the moral of the story as a conclusion to their illustrated version. An extension of the work is into pupils' own writing of another fable in either English or Scots or another language, using a source like Aesop or making up a new fable.

Products

Class illustrated version of the Henryson fable.

Pupils' own fables.

Supporting materials

Copies of Henryson fable.

Taped reading of poem.

Sources of illustrative material.

Copy of Aesop's Fables (preferably illustrated).

Scots School Dictionary and other Scots dictionaries as desired.

Other comments

Several periods will be needed to do this work properly. A positive attitude towards the difficulties presented by Henryson's language and practical ideas about how to overcome pupils' problems are essential.

EXEMPLAR 25

Level/stage of school

S3.

Duration

I or 2 periods.

Topic/Text(s)

'A Counterblaste Against Tobacco' by King James VI.

Purposes

To examine James's arguments against smoking and compare them with modern scientific arguments and publicity.

To introduce pupils to a piece of discursive Renaissance Scots prose with its features of language.

Teaching approaches

1. Introduce the topic of smoking and the arguments against it as seen in the media. Produce examples of these arguments (posters, booklets, copied extracts, etc.) and elicit reactions.

2. Supply pupils with copies of James VI's pamphlet; read and discuss it in sections to clarify the language as necessary.

3. Pupils in groups compare James's arguments with the modern ones, and evaluate him as an anti-smoking propagandist. Pupils summarise his points on a sheet and rate the merit of his arguments on a scale of I to 5.

4. Final class discussion putting all group conclusions together. Possible follow-up writing (letter to the King suggesting how he could improve his pamphlet.)

Products

Summaries and evaluations of James's arguments.

Annotations of pupil copies clarifying language.

Follow-up writing (letter, etc.).

Supporting Materials

Anti-smoking publicity leaflets, etc.

Copy of portrait of James VI to accompany copies of his pamphlet.

Other Comments

Other writings by James VI might have some classroom relevance. His treatise on witchcraft (*Daemonologie*) or his advice on government (*Basilicon Doron*) will provide interesting extracts. The way in which his language became more English after he became King of England is a useful illustration of the trend in Scottish writing after 1603.

EXEMPLAR 26

Level/stage of school

S4/5.

Duration

5 periods.

Topic/text(s)

Treatment of topic of abortion: poem, 'Stobhill' by Edwin Morgan.

Purposes

To read and appreciate a set of linked dramatic monologues in different voices.

To discuss attitudes towards abortion.

To examine varieties of language in a Scottish environment.

Teaching approaches

1. Reading of the poem could be assisted by a prepared taped reading with different voices (perhaps by members of staff). Each monologue can be read/heard by pupils and discussed before moving on to the next.

2. Discussion can be in groups, with the pupils in the roles of members of a panel enquiring into the circumstances and assessing the degree of responsibility of each speaker.

3. After each monologue is heard and discussed, there can be a wider discussion of the social, personal and religious attitudes towards abortion.

4. Possible creative writing could be the nursing sister's monologue or the Sheriff's summing up after the fatal accident enquiry. An alternative is a discursive essay on the topic of abortion, using the different arguments brought out in discussion.

5. Discussion of the language of the monologues should follow the treatment of content. The monologues can be placed on a spectrum of Scots speech from urban Scots dialect to Standard English. What does the range tell us about the speech situation in Scotland? The reasons behind the different kinds of speech should be explored.

Products

Pupils' writing on the topic of abortion.

Notes on each 'witness' made by the groups as panels of enquiry.

Language diagram, showing spectrum of Scots speech in the poem, with explanatory notes.

Supporting materials

Copies of poem for pupils.

Audio-taped reading of poem.

Help sheets on each monologue to guide group discussion.

Supplementary material from periodicals and other sources on topic of abortion.

Other comments

The topic is obviously a controversial one, and teachers will judge how to approach it in the situation of their own school and locality. A valuable outcome will be the awareness by pupils of the highly charged nature of the subject and the level of emotional and intellectual commitment on each side, leading to mutually incompatible attitudes.

7

———— • ————

CONTEMPORARY SCOTTISH FICTION IN THE UPPER SCHOOL

Anne Donovan

We know nothing in the whole range of our fictitious literature which represents such shocking pictures of the worst forms of humanity.

[The reader will be] disgusted, almost sickened by details of cruelty, inhumanity and the most diabolical hate and vengeance.

Contemporary disapproval of *Trainspotting* or *The Wasp Factory*?

No. These are typical quotations from some of the earliest reviews of *Wuthering Heights* in 1847, a reminder that literature has never been a stranger to controversy. Serious writing by definition concerns itself with issues which are not always comfortable and authors often push forward the frontiers of acceptability, something we must bear in mind in the debate surrounding the suggestion that teachers should introduce their Higher pupils to contemporary Scottish novels, many of which use strong language and deal with harsh subject matter and themes.

One of the most commonly used texts at Higher is *Sunset Song* (also reviled by many critics on its publication), yet a cursory glance through the first section of the novel alone reveals a family where the mother commits suicide, killing her unborn child and two infants because she cannot cope with the thought of bearing another child and where the father's perverted beliefs lead him to desire his own daughter and treat his son with brutality. Surely this magnificent novel, which is openly discussed in the classroom with sixteen- and seventeen-year-olds, requires as much sensitivity and frankness on the part of the teacher as any contemporary text? So why does *Sunset Song* remain such a popular choice, while many of us flinch at the thought of *The Wasp Factory*, *The Trick is to Keep Breathing* or *Trainspotting*?

Perhaps the most obvious reason is the use of strong language in many modern novels. There is no getting away from the fact that, while the issues in *Sunset Song* may be as powerful and controversial (and distasteful) as those in Kelman or Welsh, it contains less directly offensive language. This is an undoubted stumbling block to acceptance in the classroom since swearing is unacceptable in Scottish schools; under such circumstances it is hardly surprising that most teachers are wary of introducing such language into their classroom, even if it occurs in an important work of quality literature.

But can we allow ourselves to ignore some of the most serious language issues arising in modern Scottish writing? The swearing in Kelman is not an optional extra, but lies at the heart of what he is trying to do. The author has argued that there is no such thing as bad language, only verbal violence, and that the swearing is 'wallpaper', a background unnoticed by the characters. Furthermore, his radical use of the narrative voice and his search for a way to give an inner life to the kind of characters who have often been marginalised are matters demanding thoughtful discussion. Surely students capable of understanding Kelman's literary methods are mature enough to cope with the taboo language?

I would argue that as Scottish teachers we cannot ignore the greatness and variety of work being published in our country, nor its relevance to young people. In teaching literature our role is threefold: to develop the skills of literary criticism through the analysis of good writing, to foster personal and social skills through discussion of themes and issues arising from literary texts and to encourage students to see themselves as writers by offering them models and inspiration. The study of contemporary Scottish authors provides an ideal medium for each of these.

Furthermore, many of these books, including those of Irvine Welsh and Iain Banks, are exceptionally popular with teenagers, perhaps attracted by their apparently sensational nature though perhaps also because they deal with contemporary issues. Given the undoubtedly strong subject matter and language of these books, is it not better for teachers to provide a forum for their discussion than to relegate such discussion to the playground? The drug culture depicted in *Trainspotting* and *Morvern Callar* is something which will impinge directly or indirectly on the lives of most of our young people in some way, and I would suggest that it is our duty as teachers to help them to explore such issues. Violence, male–female relationships and sexuality are all recurring and usually disturbing themes in contemporary Scottish fiction, and where something disturbs, it is often a sign that it should be brought out into the light for detailed examination.

However, good teaching requires sensitive awareness of the needs and capabilities of our pupils and respect for the religious and moral beliefs of pupils and parents. Most teachers will feel that the language and subject matter of many contemporary novels are unsuitable for whole-class teaching (even if our fairy godmother replaced the dusty books at the back of the book store with a split new set of *Trainspotting*!), though some, like A. L. Kennedy's *Looking for The Possible Dance*, might prove suitable for this purpose. However, whole-class teaching is only one of the strategies we have at our disposal.

One of the ways in which we can introduce contemporary Scottish writing to our classes is through the study of selected extracts from a variety of writers. Students can be made aware of the richness and diversity of Scottish writing through discussion of different styles, themes and approaches, as well as, we hope, being inspired in their own creative writing. The study of such extracts, by fostering an interest in Scottish writers, can lead on to what can be a most fruitful approach to the study of contemporary Scottish fiction; the encouragement of pupils to use such fiction, where appropriate, for their Review of Personal Reading (RPR) or Certificate of Sixth Year Studies (CSYS) dissertation.

The RPR is an ideal vehicle for the study of contemporary Scottish fiction in the classroom, since it solves most of the difficulties inherent in whole-class teaching. No one is asked to read anything they or their parents find distasteful or inappropriate while we are able to cater for different interests and levels of maturity. Many students are naturally interested in contemporary Scottish fiction and will often choose these books if we study extracts in class and suggest possible titles. While there are many eminently suitable and interesting books from other areas of literature, and while no teacher would wish to prescribe or proscribe the student's choice, the advantages of contemporary Scottish texts are twofold: relevance to the lives of the reader and the opportunity for a genuinely personal response. If several students in the class study either the same or different Scottish texts, there is the opportunity for small-group as well as teacher-student discussion. Furthermore, there is sometimes the opportunity for contact with the author through school visits or public readings.

In my own school some of the most popular choices for RPR over the past few years have been texts written by modern Scottish authors, as have six out of eleven of this year's CSYS dissertations, including Galloway, Kennedy, Banks, Warner, McIlvanney and Spence (not all of whom would be considered contentious). The freshness and liveliness of the students' responses to these texts is evident and their enthusiasm is infectious. If you have not yet suggested contemporary Scottish fiction to your senior pupils, try it: it can reach the parts other books do not.

EXEMPLAR 27

Level/stage of school

S5.

Duration

As required.

Topic/text(s)

Short story collection: *Free Love* by Ali Smith.

Purposes

To introduce pupils to the work of a new contemporary Scottish woman writer.

Teaching approaches

1. Read and discuss the short story, 'Text for the day'. Consider to what extent it can be regarded either as realistic or as surrealistic. Discuss Melissa's state of mind and why she embarks on this new life of travel and reading and book destruction. Elicit students' reactions to the story.

2. Read another story, either 'The unthinkable happens to people every day' or 'Cold iron', and discuss in a similar way. The first presents two viewpoints, the man and the little girl, and the title has an application to both as well to a television programme. Again consider the state of mind of the main character. The second presents a young woman's view of her dead mother. Consider how she comes to have a different perception of the woman who reared her.

3. A story that you might prefer the students to read themselves is 'The world with love'. There are references in the story that you might not wish to read aloud, although they are well within the students' level of maturity to cope with.

4. Something to discuss may be the degree to which Ali Smith's writing can appeal to both male and female readers. Is her perception a significantly female one, or simply a sensitive human one?

5. Further reading of the stories can be done by the students themselves before writing a considered personal response in an essay.

Products

Students' essays on one or more of the short stories, and on the author's appeal to them as readers.

Supporting materials

A copy or copies of *Free Love* by Ali Smith, and copies of one or more stories for student reading.

Other comments

There are several new Scottish women writers worth introducing to students through their short stories, e.g. A. L. Kennedy in *Night Geometry and the Garscadden Trains*, Janice Galloway in *Blood*, or Pat Gerber in *Maiden Voyage*, etc.

EXEMPLAR 28

Level/stage of school

S5/6.

Duration

I period.

Topic/text(s)

Short story: 'Where the Debris Meets the Sea' by Irvine Welsh. NB: This story comes with a strong language health warning. Teachers must make up their minds whether they feel confident about handling it with a mature Upper School group.

Purposes

To examine the humour and implied social comment in a story by a hugely popular contemporary cult writer.

To discuss the place of strong language in a modern text.

Teaching approaches

1. Discuss with the class how glamorous images of film stars and tabloid stories of their private lives in faraway luxurious environments feed the fantasies, including sexual fantasies, of ordinary people living apparently dull and unglamorous lives in real places. Do the stars have their own fantasies?

2. Distribute photocopies of the story to the class. Let students read the story themselves and make notes about what the writer is doing with the familiar convention of 'Hello magazine'-type presentation and with the ways that men and women may talk about the opposite sex.

3. Open up the discussion to consider the sources of humour in the story. The notion of role reversal should be explored, with all the ways in which it operates in the story.

4. As the teacher feels necessary, examine how Welsh uses strong sexual language in the story to heighten the humorous incongruity of the glamorous stars discussing the young men of Leith as objects of desire. Is such language justifiable in fiction beyond such a specific literary purpose?

5. Finish by considering the implications of the title, if it has not already been done.

Products

Students' notes on the story.

Supporting materials

Photocopies of the story.

Copies of *Hello* and other gossip magazines as desired.

Other comments

This short treatment of a story may be part of an examination of the language of modern fiction and how writers do not feel bound to observe the traditional polite linguistic conventions of society. It is clearly a topic that agitates parents and authorities, giving rise to more or less successful attempts to censor literature in education. A clear acceptable policy has to be worked out if the teaching of modern literature in schools is not to be handicapped by blanket condemnations of anything that would offend the delicate.

EXEMPLAR 29

Level/stage of school

S5.

Duration

As required.

Topic/text(s)

Study of a novel: *Laidlaw* by William McIlvanney.

Purposes

To encourage students to read, reflect and write thoughtfully on a Scottish work of fiction.

To introduce students to the work of a major Scottish novelist with a view to further reading.

Teaching approaches

1. Make copies of the novel available to students and organise the reading by them in stages over a few days. The novel is not a difficult one to read and is best read as quickly as possible in the first instance to catch the flavour and pace of the narrative.

2. At an appropriate stage, after some of the reading has been done, begin a schematic representation of the plot, setting out: the main events of each day of the action from late Saturday night through to late on Tuesday night; the main characters and their relationships; and the forming of the different groups involved in the hunt for Tommy Bryson, the killer, i.e. the two investigation teams led by Laidlaw and Milligan respectively, and the two criminal groups under John Rhodes and Matt Mason, intent on hunting down Bryson and killing him. The motives and methods of each group should be discussed and notes kept by students in addition to any class charts. This representation of the plot should be maintained

until the end of the study.

3. A map of Glasgow should be provided for the physical movement of Laidlaw and the others to be followed and marked in some visible way, e.g. with pins, so the strong localising and movement of the novel can be observed in action.

4. Another dimension of the novel deserving attention is McIlvanney's use of little incidents and encounters that convey a sense of the variety and character of Glasgow, as Laidlaw says, the 'twenty-four hour cabaret'. Discuss why Laidlaw uses this technique of introducing material that does not relate to the action.

5. Discussion topics that can help to deepen awareness of the novel are: the portrayal of Laidlaw as a complex and ambiguous character inviting both admiration and criticism; the shifting narrative viewpoints of the novel from one character to another; the author's attitudes towards his characters (for instance, is there a implied admiration of the old-style gangster John Rhodes as against the modern crime boss, Matt Mason?); *Laidlaw* as a 'Whydunnit' rather than a 'Whodunnit'.

6. The usual kind of critical writing can be done on this novel; a useful comparison can be made between *Laidlaw* and other crime novels read by pupils, as well as television police series, notably STV's *Taggart*.

EXEMPLAR 30

Level/stage of school

S5/6.

Duration

As required.

Topic/text(s)

Study of novels by Iain Banks for students' Review of Personal Reading.

Purposes

To encourage the reading and appreciation of an important contemporary novelist.

To introduce students to a variety of narrative techniques and tones exhibited by a versatile and imaginative writer.

Teaching approaches

1. Make sure that a range of the novels of Iain Banks (including his science fiction novels as Iain M. Banks) are available in the school library (and class library if appropriate). Make available in the classroom a selection of comments on and reviews of Iain Banks novels, if these can be obtained. (Iain Banks's publishers, Little, Brown & Co., may supply some material on request.)

2. Conduct informal discussion with students individually or in groups to find out who has read some of Banks's work. Currently, it is quite likely that some students have read a number of his books. Encourage them to talk about the books and their reactions to them in front of the class as a whole, merely to inform others and possibly to stimulate them to read one or two Banks novels for themselves.

3. Read one or two of Banks's short stories to the class. *The State of the Art* contains mostly science fiction stories, but there is one suitable topical story, 'Piece', which deals with the Lockerbie air disaster and religious extremism. Another possible story to read is 'Road of Skulls', a humorous piece of science fiction displaying Banks's off-beat imagination. The title story, the novella 'State of the Art', is a good introduction to the main themes of Banks's earlier science fiction.

4. If possible, a couple of seminars might be set up in the class for students to give individual or group presentations on popular Banks novels, e.g. *The Wasp Factory*, *Espedair Street*, *The Bridge*, *Complicity*, etc. The occasions can serve as opportunities to 'sell' Banks as a suitable candidate for a Review of Personal Reading, as well as a good author to read for personal pleasure.

Products

One or two Reviews of Personal Reading, perhaps, but also a more general awareness of a currently popular and successful writer.

Other Comments

This approach to a writer is necessarily informal and takes account of a current fashion in adolescent reading. A similar approach might be tried with any topical writer, e.g. Irvine Welsh (at the moment of writing).

Part III The Scottish Syllabus

8

———— • ————

BEYOND THE CRINGE: USING THE EXEMPLARS AND PLANNING PROGRAMMES

Alan MacGillivray

CLEARING THE GROUND

Really there have been enough words on the matter. An extended rationale is only required for practices that are not self-evidently reasonable. The teaching of Scottish language, literature and culture is the most reasonable and natural activity for teachers to pursue in a Scottish school.

There are only three possible arguments against this practice. The first would be that Scotland is not a sufficiently identifiable national community to make the teaching of its culture valid. The second would be that Scottish literature and culture are not of sufficient merit to justify the special attention. The third would be that national origin should not be a criterion in the selection of literary texts.

The first argument is nonsense. Whatever the flawed and ridiculous constitutional situation of Scotland may be, its individual community identity has never been in question, even from the dedicated Unionist. Those who deny it are purely malicious and do not deserve our intellectual attention.

The second argument arises out of sheer ignorance. In Europe there are six great vernacular national literatures of the modern age: French, Italian, Spanish, English, German and Russian. Of all the many other smaller national literatures of Europe, Scottish literature is almost certainly the most significant in terms of longevity, variety and quality. Existing as it does in three rich and powerful languages and having been in constant touch with the central movements of European culture, it is neither limited nor parochial. Those who deny this simply do not know what they are talking about. Until they are better informed, no meaningful discussion can be held with them.

The third argument would be an appealing one in an ideal world. However, since every nation, whether long-established or recently emerged, places its own culture (including literature) in a prominent position within the educational system, there is no reason why Scotland should act differently. There is not one set of rules for Scotland and another for the rest of the world. Once there is a general movement among nations towards internationalism in cultural education, we can consider a different set of priorities. Those who seek this now are dreamers. Let us leave them.

THE WAY AHEAD

Once you step into this new and natural element, there is an exhilarating feel to the environment. It has a nipping and an eager air. The well-worn paths through other people's textual choices, the comforting fogs and recycled breath of cliché commentary, the enervating reappearance of familiar tasks like unwelcomed milestones along the rutted and muddy track of the annual syllabus: all these can be bypassed as you make your own way, walking through grass and heather for the first time. There is a new excitement, even a whiff of danger, in the wind.

That was one way of putting it – a pedantic exercise in flowery metaphor, using an outworn romantic convention. All it boils down to is that, once you go for the teaching of Scottish language and literature in a big way, all the well-established routines and conventional topics will cease to satisfy; you will get a much-needed booster jag to your professional potential, a tonic to your personal literary interests, a sharpening of your sense of intellectual adventure. There is really a whole new world out there.

Yet nothing of the familiar is really lost. I can write about these things, extol the benefits of teaching our own country's literature, and yet quite naturally employ references from Shakespeare and Eliot in my argument. As you develop an interest in teaching Scottish literature, it not only grafts on to and enriches, but also draws from and is nourished by your pre-existing tastes and resources.

Thus the way ahead into the world of Scottish literature teaching will be followed, partly as a stimulating and uncharted progress and partly as an extension to your already well-used mental maps. So this volume is not going to give you a set of fully worked out units of work that have no connection with what you are currently doing with your classes. The aims and purposes, the teaching approaches, the class and individual products and outcomes: these are not totally specific to Scottish language and literature. There are purposes and outcomes from the study of Scottish texts and topics that will be relevant within a

Scottish social and cultural context, but for the most part, what emerges from the study will be what you have always been trying to do in the English classroom. Scottish language and literature are primarily the medium and vehicle for the continuing well-defined and agreed professional intentions of the English teacher.

Consequently, we are giving you here a large and varied collection of Scottish exemplars that are sufficiently worked out for you to take on further, to flesh out, as the jargon has it, into your own classroom or departmental units and topics. More thinking and planning will have to be done on each exemplar, but we hope that the guidance given is enough for you to see an attainable and workable set of linguistic and literary activities, a worthwhile educational enterprise.

What follows is an examination of the given exemplars and other possibilities in a number of suitable learning contexts.

EXEMPLAR OF SCOTTISH TEXTS AND TOPICS

Exemplars of Literary Tradition

A currently neglected aspect of literature teaching is the placing of the texts being read by pupils within their literary and cultural context. It could be argued that this is not a vital concern, since the main interest of the teaching is more properly focused directly on the text with a view to encouraging students to read with both pleasure and alertness. However, many teachers still think it is of some importance to be aware of how a particular text sits within the literary tradition. And if the unexamined policy of the school system is still to undervalue Scottish culture and history and to make no specific place for these within the curriculum, many teachers will feel an obligation to remedy this deficiency in even a small way within their classrooms. So we have included some exemplars to encourage this practice.

Exemplars of the range and length of the Scottish literary tradition

An approach to the teaching of literature which concentrates almost exclusively on texts of the twentieth century is not calculated to give pupils any awareness of the nature of a literary tradition, any sense that a literary text is not merely the immediate product of the current moment but the result of a long process extending back through time. There is probably an unconscious assumption by many pupils that all the literature that matters is the writing of their own age, since the oldest texts that many of them read are poems of the First World War, glimpsed by them on an unspeakably remote mental horizon. The lack of a sense of history is not purely the result of their English teaching, of course, but that has made its contribution. In terms of an awareness of the validity and age of Scottish literature, a positive teaching policy that introduces pupils, gradually and probably in small doses, to older Scottish writing will be a significant help in their social and community development. From the fourteenth century onwards, there is a considerable body of Scottish writing both in prose and poetry which is a fertile mine of interesting short texts and extracts that can link up with modern concerns and illustrate that there is a shared recognisable humanity that runs through all ages and is accessible to all. From the poetry of the Makars (Exemplars 24, 31, 41) and the traditional ballads (Exemplars 5, 42), from the early Scots prose writers (Exemplars 6, 12, 13, 25) through the eighteenth-century Vernacular Revival (Exemplars 8, 43) and the greatness of Burns (Exemplars 1, 9, 34, 35, 36, 40) into the nineteenth and early twentieth centuries (Exemplars 4, 15, 45), there is a wealth of possible classroom material feasible at all stages with the right degree of thought and imagination behind their presentation. The exemplars in this volume can do no more than signal a small proportion of what is there.

With what is suggested here, a lot can be done. For example, the use of the chronicle story of King MacBeth in sources like Bellenden (Exemplar 6) and Andrew of Wyntoun (*Oxford Book of Scottish Verse*, pp. 19-22) can enhance the study of Shakespeare's *Macbeth*. Some sixteenth-century historical writing (Exemplars 12, 13) can be used as the source for a wide variety of discussion and writing in topical formats. A catalogue poem like Dunbar's 'Lament for the Makaris' can be shown visually in modern images with associated writing (Exemplar 41).

Exemplars of genre

A basic awareness of genre comes through in most school literature programmes, with the obvious distinctions between poetry and prose and drama, and the sub-distinctions of short story and novel. The variety of possible poetic forms read in school probably does not extend beyond sonnet and dramatic monologue, short free verse and occasional longer narrative. It is a moot point how much awareness of genre and form should be taught, but in a positive teaching of Scottish literature, one of the important lessons for pupils should be that Scottish writing throughout its history has exhibited as much variety of form as any other literature. So a sense of the variety of Scottish writing ought to be conveyed. The use of different poetic forms (Exemplars 4, 8, 16, 26, 31, 32, 33, 34, 35, 41, 43), the variety of length in fiction (Exemplars 3, 15, 17, 29, 36, 44, 45) and the existence of a Scottish dramatic tradition before the modern age (Exemplar 7): these can be illustrated by the use of many accessible texts.

Two forms seem particularly suitable for extended treatment. The continuing popularity of the sonnet as a manageable and comparatively accessible classic form suggests the very rich Scottish dimension of the topic. The Scottish Renaissance sonneteers, like Fowler, Montgomerie and Drummond, at the court of James VI in Scotland and later in England, deserve their place (Exemplar 32), and certainly the use of the sonnet in modern times, especially by Edwin Morgan and Robert Garioch (Exemplars 32, 33), is a rich area of work. The other especially suitable topic is the study of prose fiction of different lengths, from the short short story (as by Alasdair Gray, 'The Spread of Ian Nicol', or Tom Leonard, 'Mr Endrews Speaks', in *Streets of Stone*, eds Moira Burgess and Hamish Whyte, Edinburgh: Salamander Press, 1985) through the regular short story (as by Iain Crichton Smith, 'The Wedding', Exemplar 17, and Ali Smith in *Free Love*, Exemplar 27) to the long story and novella (as by R. L. Stevenson, 'The Bottle Imp', Exemplar 45, and *The Strange Case of Dr Jekyll and Mr Hyde*).

Exemplars of major literary periods

If the literary tradition is to be looked at specifically in the course of a literature programme, as we would argue it should, an obvious focus of attention is the sequence of natural periods, where the writers tend to exhibit some common characteristics or simply in aggregate add up to a significant identifiable group or constellation. In the Scottish literary tradition, the received wisdom is that there are three great periods that deserve to be honoured by serious consideration: the pre-Union period of the writers associated with the Stewart court, loosely referred to as the period of the Makars (Exemplars 7, 12, 13, 18, 24, 25, 31, 32, 41); the period of the Scottish Enlightenment with the great novelists, Scott, Galt and Hogg (not represented in exemplars here), and the Vernacular Revival poets (Exemplars 1, 8, 9, 34, 35, 36, 43); and the twentieth century, beginning with the Scottish Renaissance associated with Hugh MacDiarmid, Lewis Grassic Gibbon and others (Exemplars

2, 4, 47, 48) up to the more recent post-1945 writers (Exemplars 4, 16, 17, 22, 23, 26-30, 44, 49). Apparently less rich periods or stages, like the nineteenth-century Kailyard or the seventeenth-century period of religious dissension, can be identified but there is so much revaluation of these periods going on that it would be dangerous to make generalisations about their relatively lesser importance.

Exemplars of great names in literature

In the older kind of literary criticism that formed the mental map of literature for most school and university students down to comparatively recent times, the literary tradition was rather like a landscape dotted with hills and landmarks of differing degrees of eminence: poets, novelists, dramatists, men (almost invariably) of letters. From the number and disposition of these in time and space, it was possible to reach some kind of conclusion about the international importance of the national tradition. So the English tradition came out at the top of the league of big names: QED. The purpose of the big Scottish names was to add necessary weight to this prize contender, and Scott, Burns, Stevenson, with Henryson and Dunbar as more dubious followers of Chaucer, had their individual places in the standard literary histories.

They should have their place also in the developing sense of the Scottish literary tradition. Whatever the fashionable critical theory or the critical orthodoxy may be, the student emerging from school and university should have at least a nodding acquaintance with, and preferably some more direct experience of, the writers whose contributions have been most notable. Within each of the significant periods of the Scottish literary tradition, there are names that students can associate with it. The figures of Robert Henryson and William Dunbar, and probably David Lyndsay, the most popular Scottish writer before the time of Burns, should be in their consciousness from the age of the Makars (Exemplars 7, 24, 31, 41). The Enlightenment should call to their minds the names of Robert Fergusson and Robert Burns as poets and Walter Scott, John Galt and James Hogg as prose writers, with R. L. Stevenson as a major Victorian (Exemplars 1, 8, 9, 34, 35, 36, 40, 45). In the twentieth century, Hugh MacDiarmid and Sorley MacLean are essential poets, with Lewis Grassic Gibbon (Exemplars 2, 47, 48) and Neil Gunn as novelists and James Bridie in drama.

Exemplars of Critical Approaches to Literature

What has gone before represents a study of Scottish literature in terms of the traditional attitudes and contextualising approaches of historical criticism. If Scottish literature is to be appreciated as a significant entity within the wider social and cultural tradition, as it assuredly must be if its identity and coherence are to be understood, this approach must underpin any study of Scottish texts. Nevertheless, as any student of modern literary thinking will readily argue, it is only one of many ways of looking at text. In this volume and its companions, we have, probably for the first time in an educational work at the school level, set out to look at how Scottish texts can be studied in the light of some of the influential later twentieth-century critical approaches. Two of our contributors, Douglas Gifford and James McGonigal, argue for new ways of reading Scottish literature, particularly at the Upper School stage. In the light of their chapters, there are a number of exemplars provided to allow teachers and senior students to engage with aspects of criticism like feminist criticism (Exemplar 1), Marxist criticism (Exemplar 2), reader-response theory (Exemplar 3), influence and intertextuality (Exemplar 4), and Bakhtinian theory of the dialogic novel (Exemplar 47). These do not go very far or very deeply into the issues, but they represent a first stage in what is possible with school groups. An indispensable source of reference and workbook for teachers in this area is, of course, *Literary Studies in Action* (A. Durant and N. Fabb, London: Routledge, 1990), in which the whole field of the reading and analysis of texts is surveyed and exemplified. A vast amount of work waits to be done in the application of these techniques to Scottish writers and texts. The opening up of Scottish writing with the tools of modern critical theory will undoubtedly be interesting and rewarding.

Exemplars of Language

It is a truism to say that any classroom lesson is in some sense a lesson in language. The old attitude of the maths teacher who said, 'We don't use language in our subject', ought to have disappeared up the parallel lines to infinity. Whatever doubt some subject teachers may have about their function as teachers of language (and there is a whole book to be written about the role of all teachers as teachers of Scottish language), there can be no arguing against the fact that any study of literature necessarily involves the study and use not only of the language of the text, but also of the languages brought by the teacher and the pupils to that text. George Sutherland, in an earlier chapter, stressed the need to avoid looking at the language of Scottish literature 'as if it were a dead language existing only in written form.' So, in any of the exemplars in this volume, there is an implicit linguistic dimension of an active kind. All the language displayed in the texts was and is a real language such as Scots do use, and a major part of the literature study is the discovery of that quality of living in the words on the page.

Over and above that obligation on the teacher to make each lesson a language study, there is the further need to promote a greater awareness by the pupils of the languages in use around them in Scotland and as used by themselves and their families. So we have provided a number of exemplars specifically on language issues, mainly on Scots of different types depending on its time and place, but also on Gaelic and English as used by Scottish speakers and writers. From the study of language in the community (Exemplar 10) and in literature (Exemplars 19, 26) to the discovery by pupils of their own linguistic history (Exemplar 39); from a general extension of vocabulary (Exemplars 20, 38) to the observation of words in use for specific purposes (Exemplars 14, 21); from specific study of the different local forms of language (using *The Kist* - Exemplar 37) to a survey of a linguistic condition like bilingualism (Exemplar 22): the exemplars provided here allow a beginning to a systematic study of the Scottish language situation. And it would be wise to see the allocation of these exemplars to particular school stages as being very notional. Any of the topics introduced can be dealt with at any stage of the school using materials of appropriate sophistication.

There is a need for a more graded and systematic approach to the study of Scottish language in Scottish schools. However, as yet we lack some essential instruments: a new grammar of Scots to document clearly the historical and other valid differences in expression that exist between Scots and its sister language of English and within Scots between its different dialects; a related survey of the markers of Scottish Standard English as distinct from other standard forms of English (Southern, American, Irish, etc.); and materials on Gaelic that describe it clearly to the non-speaker and non-learner. Without these, the non-specialist is moving in an uncharted area and is prey to many ignorant misconceptions, prejudices and social propaganda deceptions. Phrases like 'Scottish (or Glasgow) slang', 'lazy urban speech', 'the real Doric', 'speaking properly', 'bad grammar', 'teuchter talk' and many others display the sad level of nonsensical prattle that passes for serious comment on language even among educated people in Scotland today.

THE CORE SCOTTISH SYLLABUS

Once you begin on a policy of teaching Scottish texts and topics as a regular part of your classroom work, you have taken a very significant step along a clear road that lies before you. Unless you deliberately rule out logic and rational thinking from your mental processes and, as it were, turn aside from the road or turn back, or erect a mental roadblock to prevent further progress, you will naturally go on to apply an ever-increasing measure of planning into your use of these texts and topics. There will be a growing coordination of them within your overall purposes so that you move more and more towards the deliberate creation of a syllabus that depends more and more upon Scottish elements within it. From there it is but a short logical step to the syllabus that has the Scottish element at its core. Whatever size that core may be, and it will inevitably vary from school to school, the planning will begin with the Scottish texts and topics and move outwards to encompass the other necessary elements (English, American, European, etc.). No other approach seems to have any logical basis within a programme of teaching Scottish pupils within the schools of Scotland.

There is a kind of Renaissance moment implicit in this. Under the old 'Ptolemaic' system of literature education, Scottish literature hung suspended from the great Paradise of English literature, lower in position and worth, encased in its own planetary spheres of language and culture, given life by the 'primum mobile' of English. A few blessed souls might aspire to be received within the English heaven above, saved by their purging of coarser Scottish qualities and worthy to be admitted to the syllabus. All else was in grave danger of being plunged into the lower depths, damnation in an uncouth Hell of dialect versifiers and urban novelists, where the atmosphere is lurid with Scotticisms and sexual obscenities. Under this system, Scottish texts had to prove themselves able to meet externally created criteria of harmonisation with non-Scottish texts; they were marginalised within their own territory, peripheral in their own cosmos.

The new philosophy that rightly calls this in doubt is a 'Copernican' revolution in thinking. A clearer view of the skies reveals that the reality requires a different description, the education structure demands a different set of priorities. The vitality and strength of Scottish literature and culture give them a rightful place at the centre of their system, a sun around which revolve the complementary and, in their own ways, essential planets of other literary and cultural elements. In the language and literature syllabus in Scottish schools, Scottish literature is the natural and central sun, and other literatures occupy secondary and supporting roles, vital in their own distinctive contributions but not displacing Scottish culture from its position at the heart. Moving outward from this heart, the planning priorities are: Scottish language, literature and culture; literature in other related language forms - English, American, Irish, etc.; European literature in translation; world literature in general. No one of these monopolises the syllabus; no one of them is ignored. A genuine internationalism growing out of an awareness of our own culture rightly supplants the parochialism of an external culture.

AN OUTLINE SCOTTISH SYLLABUS

It is not possible here to do more than outline some of the apparent necessary ingredients of a Scottish syllabus at the different stages of the school. It is, for convenience, divided into the stages: 5–14 (a) Primary and (b) Lower Secondary, Middle Secondary, and Upper Secondary. There is a distinction made between *Input* (Language, Literature and History/Culture) and *Output* (Writing, Talk and Products).

5–14 (a) Primary

Input

Language:

> Awareness of the variety of Scottish voices.
> Formation of open accepting attitude to different accents and forms of speech.

Literature:

> Reading of different forms of Scots in verse and prose (poems, ballads, stories).
> Reading of appropriate Scottish children's fiction.
> Use of anthology and teaching approaches in *The Kist*, etc.

History/Culture

> Awareness of main regions of Scotland.
> Important facts of Scottish history.
> Listening to Scottish songs and music.
> Looking at Scottish art and photographs.

> Stories and poems using Scots words.

Talk:

> Talking about stories etc. that have been read.
> Talking about family events and members, personal experiences, etc., using natural expression.

Products:

> Materials for display.
> Audio tape-recordings.
> Class magazine, anthology of writing.

5–14 (b) Lower Secondary (Stages 1/2)

Input

Language:

> More work on Scottish voices.
> Use of Scots and Gaelic dictionaries.
> Awareness of languages of Scotland.
> Scots proverbs and sayings, street games and rhymes.

Literature:

> Scots poems and ballads, including Burns.
> Scottish stories – folktales, short stories.
> Appropriate Scottish children's fiction.

History/Culture

> Geographical and cultural areas of Scotland.
> Basic outline of Scottish history from the beginnings.
> Scots and Gaelic songs.
> Scottish painting (as discussion and writing stimulus).

Writing in Scots (anecdotes, jokes, verse, etc.).
Stories and dramatic sketches on Scottish themes (ballad stories, modern situations using a variety of Scottish tones, e.g. in dialogue).
Conversion of Standard English texts (e.g. notices, newspaper reports, radio items) into Scots.

Talk:

Discussions in local speech (e.g. of texts read, of local events, etc.).
Storytelling in Scots.
Dramatisation of ballads, etc.

Products:

Taped radio programmes.
Video of class presentation.
Dramatic presentations.
Class episodic novel.

Middle Secondary (Stages 3/4)

Input

Language:

Study of local dialect (in speech and writing).
Using a Scots dictionary in personal writing.
Awareness of Scottish Standard English (using radio, speakers, etc.).
Writing in Scots/Gaelic, or using Scots/Gaelic elements in a writing context.
Study of Scottish place names and surnames.

Literature:

Short stories, novella.
Scottish poems (e.g. Burns and Standard Habbie, Scottish war poetry, modern poets, a few Older Scots poems or extracts).
A short Scottish play.

History/Culture:

> Scottish media (popular press, television series, radio programmes).
> Modern Scotland as shown on television or in film.
> Modern Scottish popular music (rock, modern folksong).
> Scottish historical myths.

Output

Writing:

> Narrative and descriptive writing in Scots and Scottish Standard English.
> Dramatic scripts for recording.
> Discursive writing using some Scots vocabulary and idiom.

Talk:

> Discussion in Scottish Standard English and local dialect (topical issues, texts, etc.).
> Prepared items for reading and recording.
> Dramatising texts etc.

Products

> Radio programme.
> Display, dramatic presentation.
> Video programme.
> Class anthology of writing.

Upper Secondary (Stages 5/6)

Input

Language:

> An awareness of Older Scots and Gaelic.
> Informed study of attitudes to Scottish language in society.
> Study of the use of Scottish language in the media.

Literature:

> Awareness of the Scottish literary tradition.
> A modern Scottish novel (and/or novelist).

A classical Scottish novel (or novelist).
Extended personal reading of Scottish texts.
Modern poets.
A group of pre-twentieth-century Scots poems.
A piece of Scottish drama.

History/Culture:

Scotland in history (fact and fiction).
Scottish art as a set of images of Scottish life.
Scotland in film.

Output

Writing:

Discursive writing on important topics (bringing out the Scottish
dimension).
Practical criticism from Scottish sources.
Critical writing using Scottish vocabulary and idiom.
Creative writing using Scottish literary stimulus.

Talk:

General discussion of Scottish topics (literary, linguistic, cultural,
topical).

Products:

Group project on drama or a major Older Scots text.
Video programme.
Creative writing submitted for publication.

The foregoing suggestions can represent only a very generalised
outline of a core Scottish syllabus. The normal factors of time,
availability of resources, special circumstances of the school and pupil
population must be significant. However, the limitations must be seen
as only modifying factors reducing or qualifying or altering the
composition of the core syllabus, not ruling it out. It is our contention
that some form of core Scottish syllabus is always possible, is possible
now, and that the tendency through the experience of planning,
resourcing and implementing it will be for it to develop and grow. A
Scottish syllabus in language and literature is a natural and rational
element within the curriculum of a Scottish school. The attitudes of
prejudice, of ignorance or of despair that give rise to a resistance to the

idea are there only in the short term, and we cannot allow them to dictate indefinitely the way in which Scottish pupils experience their inherited culture.

EXEMPLAR 31

Level/stage of school

S5/6.

Duration

2 or 3 periods.

Topic/text(s)

Literature study: a moral fable, 'The Two Mice' or 'The Taill of the Uponlandis Mous and the Burges Mous', by Robert Henryson.

Purposes

To study an Older Scots classic text for examination purposes.

To become aware of the rich literary and linguistic tradition of medieval and Renaissance Scotland, not only through this text but also through reference to others by Henryson and his followers.

Teaching approaches

1 Introduce the topic of fables with reference to well-known examples of stories with morals; read one or two of Aesop's fables. Introduce also the idea of stories with animals acting like humans (e.g. George Orwell's *Animal Farm*, Disney cartoons, Tom and Jerry cartoons, Bugs Bunny, folktales like Brer Rabbit stories, etc.

2. Refer to medieval fondness for this kind of story, as shown in the beast epic 'Le Roman de Renart' with its stories of the cunning fox and other animals; introduce the poet Robert Henryson, a schoolmaster in Dunfermline, and his Moral Fables based on Aesop and the Reynard stories.

3. Read the fable 'The Two Mice' (with the help of a taped reading, if

desired). Discuss topics arising from the reading: the 'Rime Royal' stanza form; the Scots language forms (see the Introduction in the *Concise Scots Dictionary* for information about Older Scots grammar and vocabulary etc.); the characterisation of the two sister mice with different lifestyles and expectations; the vividness of the descriptions and the vigour of the action culminating in the near death of the country mouse and her escape back home; the mirroring of real Scottish society with the division between traditional poor rural life and the new material comforts of the rising towns; and the appropriateness of Henryson's 'moralitas' (moral), if it is provided in the text.

4. Pupils write a critical essay on the poem, covering a set of chosen points, with a personal response.

Products

Pupils' writings on the poems.

Notes on the poem covering content, message and language.

Supporting materials

Scots dictionary.

Notes on Older Scots language.

Background material on Henryson.

Selected fables by Aesop and other writers (e.g. La Fontaine).

Other comments

This is one of the most immediately accessible fables of Henryson, because it is such a well-known story. Other Henryson fables worth studying for this reason are 'The Lion and the Mouse' and 'The Cock and the Fox' (the latter contains some bawdy dialogue among the hens).

EXEMPLAR 32

Level/stage of school

S4/5.

Duration

4/5 periods.

Topic/text(s)

The sonnet in Scottish poetry: sonnets by the poets of the Castalian Band, poets of the court of James VI; modern sonnets by Robert Garioch, George Mackay Brown and Edwin Morgan.

Purposes

To make pupils aware that there is a tradition of sonnet writing in Scottish poetry as well as in English and other European poetry.

To introduce pupils to the idea of the sonnet sequence as a poetic form for developing a train of thought on a topic.

Teaching approaches

1. Supply copies of the sonnets: 'In Orknay' (William Fowler); 'First, Jove, as greatest god above the rest' (James VI); 'To his Mistress' (Alexander Montgomerie); 'O cruell love, why dothe thow sore assayle' from 'The Tarantula of Love' (William Fowler); 'The tender snow, of granis soft and quhyt' (Alexander Montgomerie) - see Appendix C.

2. Read the sonnets quickly and without lingering on complete explanation and analysis. The point is to observe that these are sonnets from a group of Renaissance Scottish poets under the king's patronage dealing with conventional subjects like love and poetry. The form of the sonnet used in these examples is worth studying. It is not the common Petrarchan or Shakespearian forms used by English poets of the same period. The rhyme scheme is abab bcbc cdcd ee, a tighter and more demanding scheme than the Shakespearian form which it to some extent resembles. It seems to have been the favourite form within this particular poetic group. Like the sonneteers of Renaissance England - Shakespeare, Spenser, Sidney, etc. - the Scots poets tended to write sequences of sonnets. William Fowler's sequence is entitled 'The Tarantula of Love', suggesting the maddening poisonous nature of strong love passion. This is worth pointing out in passing to pupils.

3. The main part of the sonnet study should be devoted to modern Scottish poets. Sonnets by Robert Garioch and Edwin Morgan can be the main focus: some of Robert Garioch's Edinburgh sonnets can be found in a

number of anthologies, notably the *Faber Book of Twentieth-Century Scottish Poetry*; Edwin Morgan's Glasgow Sonnets can be found in *Selected Poems of Edwin Morgan*. Garioch's wry and reductive humour makes his sonnets very readable, though his use of Scots needs some language work. Morgan's 'Glasgow Sonnets' are worth looking at as a unity, presenting Morgan's thoughts on the changes he observes taking place in his home city. A single sonnet worth reading is the well-known poem 'The Old Women' by George Mackay Brown, which is not usually observed to be a sonnet.

EXEMPLAR 33

Level/stage of school

S5/6.

Duration

4/5 periods.

Topic/text(s)

Study of a major sonnet sequence: *Sonnets from Scotland* by Edwin Morgan.

Purposes

To study a major poetic work by a contemporary poet.

To examine the use of the sonnet form applied in a new imaginative way to a major topic.

Teaching approaches

1. Provide copies of the whole sequence of sonnets (51 sonnets) for pupil work individually and in groups.

2. Read selected sonnets to establish the narrative situation of the work: Scotland being observed by unidentified beings from elsewhere in the universe throughout the centuries from the remote beginnings to the present and on into the remotest future. 'Slate' and 'Carboniferous' deal with the beginnings; 'Travellers (1)' suggests the moving from Scotland

out into the universe and back; 'A Golden Age' and 'The Summons' deal with the ending. Discuss the imaginative concept behind the sequence and what it suggests about Morgan's attitude to Scotland.

3. Set up students to read and discuss a range of sonnets on aspects of the past, present and possible futures of Scotland. Suggested examples are: 'Pilate at Fortingall', 'At Stirling Castle, 1507', 'Theory of the Earth' for the past; 'Gangs' and 'Not the Burrell Collection' for the present; 'The Age of Heracleum', 'Computer Error: Neutron Strike', 'The Coin' and 'The Solway Canal' for visions of the future.

4. Other topics worth looking at come into the sequence', e.g. the Scottish poets in North Africa during the Second World War in 'North Africa'; the poet himself at work in 'The Poet in the City'; the danger of having nuclear submarine bases on the Clyde and being a strategic target. These can be separately studied if desired. At some point the students should read all the sonnets themselves as a sequence to get a sense of its total effect.

5. The sonnet form as used in the sequence should be studied in some detail. How does Morgan use the form? Is he consistent throughout? How does he obtain a great variety of effects within a short restrictive form?

6. To conclude the study, students can do some critical writing in an essay. However, there should also be the opportunity for students to write sonnets of their own, perhaps their own variations and additions to the theme of Morgan's sequence.

Products

Students' notes on the sonnets and the work as a whole.

Critical essays and students' own sonnets.

EXEMPLAR 34

Level/stage of school

S5/6.

Duration

6+ periods.

Topic/text(s)

A study of Robert Burns's Satires: 'To a Louse', 'To a Haggis', 'Holy Willie's Prayer', 'The Twa Dogs'.

Purposes

To make the pupils aware of the important strain of satire in Burns's writing directed against a number of social targets.

To study the techniques by which Burns attacks different targets while generally retaining the quality of good humour and compassion.

Teaching approaches

1. The poems are taught in the normal manner, using both whole-class and group methods to inform about context and background, and to discuss the content and ideas.

2. Any or all of the poems can be the subject of necessary critical essays by the pupils.

3. This particular selection of poems enables a look at four different targets of Burns's satire: social pretension, boastful patriotism, religious hypocrisy and abuses of privilege and position.

   'To a Louse' mocks pride and showing off by setting the insignificant presumptuous louse against the finery and conceit of the young lady in church, especially her fashionable balloon-shaped headgear. Hidden within it are references that reveal Burns's familiarity with the philosophy of Adam Smith's *Theory of Moral Sentiments*.

   'To a Haggis' is not usually regarded as a satire, which probably says a lot about the skill of the technique: Burns is clearly sympathetic towards his fellow Scots in their attachment to their home-grown culture and products, but gently mocks their tendency to over-praise and exaggerate the worth of these over anything else in the world. (We have to remember that in the days before Burns Suppers, the haggis had no special place as a Scottish cultural icon - the irony is that Burns's brilliant half-mocking celebration of it has conferred a posthumous validity on his exaggerations.)

   'Holy Willie's Prayer' is a very familiar and deservedly popular poem for teaching. A point often overlooked in studying it is that Burns is not taking a daring radical stance in mocking Holy Willie, but reflecting the opinion not only of most of the people but also of the Moderate (New Licht) clergy appointed by the landowners. In social and church terms, it is Holy Willie who expresses the views of a radical fundamentalist minority, a group who fifty years later are to split the Established Church and set up a more democratic Free Church.

'The Twa Dogs' is an example of Burns's satire in a different verse form from the Standard Habbie; it is cast in the form of an eclogue, deriving from the pastoral convention of having shepherds comment satirically on the fashions and customs of polite society in a verse dialogue. Again it is interesting to note that Burns's apparent solution is not revolutionary (this poem was written before the French Revolution) but a rather conservative return to traditional Tory rural paternalism. (Burns was careful about the reactions of his readers, as in 'The Cotter's Saturday Night'.)

Products

Pupils' critical writings on chosen poem(s).

Pupils' notes.

Supporting materials

A good biography of Burns for reference.

Background historical and social material.

Taped readings of poems.

Specially prepared study materials, e.g. the Burns study guide by John Hodgart.

Other comments

There are other Burns satires that deserve study, e.g. 'Death and Doctor Hornbook', 'The Holy Fair', 'Address of Beelzebub', etc. Probably four poems is as much as a single class study can bear. Teachers should choose a group according to their preferences and purposes.

EXEMPLAR 35

Level/stage of school

S5.

Duration

4 periods.

Topic/text(s)

The study of a major long poem: 'Tam O'Shanter' by Robert Burns.

Purposes

To read a humorous narrative poem with enjoyment and to think about how the poet achieves his humorous effects.

To consider how the poem contains within it a variety of sophisticated elements that make it much more than a straightforward story of the supernatural.

Teaching approaches

1. Read the poem in the normal way, or listen to a good rendering on audio cassette. Discuss the story and the presentation of the supernatural in humorous mode.

2. Take up any or all of the following topics as desired: the treatment of social drinking in the poem; the treatment of marriage and sex in the poem (Kate, Nannie, the landlady); the attitudes towards women revealed in the poem; elements of Calvinism and traditional superstition complementing or conflicting with each other; the Scots and English elements in the poem (language, poetic sources, national feelings, etc.).

3. Pupils do follow-up critical writing as required practice and preparation for the external examinations.

Products

Pupils' formal writings on the poem.

Pupils' own notes on the poem and associated topics.

Supporting materials

There are a number of good study aids to work on 'Tam O'Shanter', notably *Robert Burns* by Kenneth Simpson and *Robert Burns: Study Guide for Revised Higher* by John Hodgart.

A good biography of Burns is needed for reference.

A useful accompanying text is Robert Burns's 'Letter to Captain Francis Grose' (CL 557–9) giving different stories about witches associated with Alloway Kirk.

Other comments

Other poems that might be read in association with 'Tam O'Shanter' are 'Address to the Deil' (Robert Burns), 'Dance of the Sevin Deidly Synnis' (William Dunbar) and 'The Witch of Fife' (James Hogg).

EXEMPLAR 36

Level/stage of school

S4/5.

Duration

3 periods.

Topic/text(s)

Comparison of two letters by Robert Burns, a prose letter and a verse epistle: 'Letter to Mrs Dunlop', 22 March 1787; 'Epistle to William Simson', May 1785.

Purposes

To make pupils aware of Robert Burns as a writer of both prose letters and verse epistles to a wide circle of friends and acquaintances.

To examine how Burns presents himself in different ways to different types of people, and how he adopts a suitable 'dramatic' role as appropriate.

Teaching approaches

1. Supply pupils with copies of the letter and the poem. Read the 'Letter to

Mrs Dunlop' first, and have pupils in groups discuss what the letter probably tells us about the writer and the recipient. Pupils can go on to discuss how Burns seems to be presenting himself to Mrs Dunlop, what impression he wishes to give about himself and possible reasons for this.

2. Read the 'Epistle to William Simson' in class. Discuss with the class the progress of the thought in the poem and how this epistle differs from a normal prose letter. In groups pupils can compare the epistle with the letter to Mrs Dunlop, deciding how it differs both in tone and attitude. Both letters deal with Burns's thoughts about himself as a poet; do they reveal different conflicting views or is there a basic consistency? What different Robert Burnses are created in the two letters?

3. Follow-up work might involve: writing a summary of each letter for comparison; writing a prose version of the letter to William Simson, if only to gain a sense of the greater concision of the verse; writing a third letter as if by Burns to some real person of today, describing himself as a poet.

Products

Pupils' annotated copies of the Burns letters.

Pupils' writings as follow-up to the study of the texts.

Supporting materials

A good Burns biography for reference.

Other comments

These two letters deal with one aspect of Burns's life. Other letters and verse epistles can be found to reveal other aspects and other roles that Burns adopts to suit his correspondent.

Part IV Stages of the School

9

———— • ————

CONFRONTING DISSONANCES: SCOTTISH LITERATURE AND LANGUAGE IN THE PRIMARY AND EARLY SECONDARY SCHOOL

Gordon Gibson and Anne Gifford

A number of important ideas about language in education have come into common currency in the 1990s. More is now known about the value for pupils of multi-dialectalism, and the barriers to their learning which can result from the denial of worth to the language of the home. The significance has been recognised of metacognition, across the entire development of literacy, and specifically in relation to awareness of, and knowledge about, language itself. Perspectives derived from media studies have helped teachers identify the importance of pupils' critical engagement with aspects of popular culture. These ideas, alongside long accepted views about the worth of the study of literature and language in general, formed a basis for *National Guidelines: English Language 5–14* (SOED, 1991).

This document marked the first ever attempt by the Scottish Office Education Department to codify the entire English Language curriculum in the primary school and the early stages of secondary school, within a single coherent statement. It came in the wake of long and sometimes bitter argument about standards of education throughout Britain. However, there has been a generally consensual approach to curriculum development in Scotland, and the guidelines, while not without their critics, did set a national agenda for English Language education, and have had a major effect on thinking, particularly in the primary sector. This has happened without the polarised arguments which have characterised curriculum change elsewhere in Britain.

Many teachers expressed pleasure that, given the debates about the position of Standard English which raged south of the border during the formulation of the National Curriculum for England and Wales, the Scottish Guidelines contained a section in which 'Scottish culture' was promoted as a 'specific issue in English Language teaching'.

This part of the guidelines, encouraging teachers to develop pupils' awareness of Scottish languages and culture, was generally well received in Scottish schools, and was perceived as relatively unproblematic. The proposals on 'good classroom practice' did not conflict with the consensus within the teaching profession. There was reassurance about the value of the 'language of the home', which for most Scottish pupils is likely to include features identifiable as Scottish in accent, lexis, syntax and idiom. The study of literature as a way of promoting pupils' personal development, strongly supported in the Guidelines, was already accepted in both primary and secondary schools.

Thus the National Guidelines 5–14 sought to provide a synthesis of the new with the tried and tested. Their potential for promoting ground-breaking work in primary schools, and in the first two years of secondary schools is enthusiastically outlined by Gordon Liddell in the first edition of *Laverock* (a magazine for teachers published by the Association for Scottish Literary Studies, and itself an indicator of the increasing interest in Scottish language and culture). While acknowledging the length of time likely to be required in order to bring about the developments that the Guidelines suggest, Liddell is unfailingly optimistic in his encouragement to the teaching profession to 'get wired in' (Liddell, 1995).

AFTER THE GUIDELINES – ENTHUSIASTS AND OTHERS

In the period immediately following the publication of the National Guidelines, local authorities and individual schools looked for support and assistance with developing policies and practices in a number of aspects of the English Language curriculum. To those involved in responding to such requests, the relative degrees of urgency provided an interesting index of the level of unfamiliarity of the ideas, or at least of the extent to which practitioners felt lacking in confidence about meeting the demands of the guidelines through current practices.

Most urgent needs seemed to focus on assessment structures, writing development and reading for information. However, requests for 'something about Scottish culture' began quite quickly to appear.

Early work took the form of one-day in-service courses, run by local authorities. Teachers were required to apply for places. The feedback from some teachers in Strathclyde schools was illuminating. Some were, indeed, willing to take forward the proposals into their own teaching, but they had already begun to identify a number of challenges which seemed to be holding them back: they felt it to be difficult to find suitable textual materials; they were often uncertain of their own knowledge about Scottish varieties of language; and they felt anxious about the attitudes of parents and colleagues towards an expansion of work in Scottish literature and, especially, in Scottish language.

To the above list, from the perspective of course organisers would have to be added the challenge arising from divided and dissonant views held by teachers about the valuing of Scottish language features in pupils' speech, and the need for advice about teaching approaches which would help pupils to develop the critical reflection suggested by the Guidelines.

Later, when opportunities arose for work with the whole staff of individual schools, the range of opinions was even wider, and statements were sometimes blunt:

'Damned nationalism by another name.'

'I've spent my career so far helping children *not* to speak like that.'

'If they can't speak English, they can't write English and they won't get on.'

While these views may not have been representative, they clearly suggested an unease among teachers about the implications of putting into practice the ideas of the Guidelines about Scottish language and culture. What had seemed a welcome and unproblematic exhortation to give Scottish culture its place, had turned into a demand which may run counter to deeply held beliefs and values. Having reached this point, teachers really begin to grapple with the full intellectual and pedagogic challenges implied in statements such as the following:

Teachers should help pupils to recognise themselves, and be able to look at themselves as Scots in a detached and self-aware manner. (SOED, 1991)

Society gives prestige to some accents and dialects, and undervalues others. Teachers will be confronted with difficult decisions: for example, what is appropriate? when should inappropriate language be corrected? (SOED, 1991)

Scottish writing and writing about Scotland should permeate the curriculum and be introduced from an early stage, taking its place beside English Literature. The objective of this is to value and examine critically the ideas, beliefs and emotions of Scottish writers, and to set them against the different insights and perspectives of writers from other places and other times. (SOED, 1991)

THE CHALLENGES

The challenges for primary and secondary schools are different. In secondary schools with specialist teachers, subject knowledge is stronger. University courses in Scotland have increasingly included study of Scottish texts. Encouragement has been given by the Scottish Examination Board for the use of Scottish materials in the upper stages of secondary schools. The work of the Association for Scottish Literary Studies has provided a steady transfusion of support materials for work in the upper secondary school. Difficulties have existed, most noticeably in finding suitable texts for S1 and S2 classes, but such texts are increasingly coming into print, and the recent publication of *The Kist/A' Chiste* (SCCC, 1996) has extended the available range.

For primary teachers, support has been less. Pre-service training, because of the breadth of curriculum to be covered, has tended not to focus specifically on issues of Scottish language and literature. An excellent discussion paper from SCOLA (Scottish Committee on Language Arts) raised the issue of *Scottish English: The Language Pupils Bring to School* (SCCC, 1980), but this was a solitary piece of curricular advice to primary schools on this aspect of language teaching. There has been a lack of a definite agenda such as the Scottish Examination Board has set for secondary schools.

The work of the Burns Federation, through its annual competition, has at least ensured that pupils in Scotland's primary schools have encountered texts which are written in Scottish dialects, but a limited range of texts has often meant a potential for 'couthiness' and has confirmed the notion of Scottish materials being in some way exotic and marginalised from the 'normal' curriculum.

Sometimes a genuine willingness to engage in some way with Scottish literature and language has resulted in the use of texts unsuitable because of their difficulty, or the presentation of texts without necessary contextualisation or support being provided for pupils. Each January, thousands of primary pupils, some as young as eight years old, sit through 'Tam O'Shanter' or 'To A Mouse' as if caught in some strange and incomprehensible national ritual. Yet the intention is sound.

Scottish language presents an even more complex set of issues. The National Guidelines are here somewhat ambivalent, requiring teachers to value pupils' spoken language and to introduce them 'to stories, poems and other texts which use dialect in a positive way', but at the same time acknowledging that 'society gives prestige to some accents and dialects, and undervalues others' (SOED, 1991). In fact, the advice stops short of addressing this central difficulty, suggesting only that pupils should be helped to develop awareness of when it is 'appropriate' for different varieties of language to be used. This is an area of live debate. For some teachers, 'Scottish language' is a term which describes a dialect continuum, including ancient and little-used features and today's much maligned urban varieties. For others, it is a distinct language kept from its rightful role in society by political as well as social values. 'Appropriateness' is a slippery term. Dialect may be seen as suitable only for informal contexts. Scots may be seen as a language fit to be used in the most formal discourses.

Even within the society of the school, knowledge about the history of Scots as a language in its own right may not be widespread. A recent survey of a sample of ninety-three Scottish secondary teachers of English found that only twenty-four had done any study of Scots language at university (Lorvik, 1995).

Nor can teachers live their lives solely within the society of the school. Any survey of the social backgrounds of teachers will show them to have come largely from those sections of society which have gained most over the years from a movement towards dominant linguistic forms and away from local or dialectal forms, certainly in their professional if not their private lives. For primary teachers in particular, depending on where they trained and their route of entry, their studies will probably not have provided them with a grounding in even the basic concepts of linguistics, such is the necessary load of other content in courses. They are unlikely to have made any specific study of the languages of Scotland, their histories and their relationships to English, or of the socio-linguistic context, through which the overlay of value judgements about language-in-use can be recognised, understood and perhaps even resisted.

Therefore, teachers wishing to confront the task of meeting the demands of the National Guidelines have to ask themselves a number of difficult questions:

> What is my understanding of, and attitude towards, the historical and linguistic background of Scottish texts?
>
> What is my own evaluative framework for selecting Scottish texts suitable for the ages and stages of the pupils I am teaching?
>
> Am I carrying unresolved dissonances between my belief in the place of Scottish literature and language in the curriculum, and my emotional responses to the dialects and accents of the spoken language of my pupils?

How do I engage in discussion with my fellow teachers and pupils' parents, so as to make clear my reasons for valuing Scottish language and literature in the curriculum?

These are challenging questions, but they must be addressed if policies are to be developed and meaningful work is to take place in the classrooms of Scottish schools.

IN THE PRIMARY CLASSROOM

It is important that children in the primary school are encouraged, from the start, to explore their own language and culture. If pupils do not acquire from their primary education an enjoyment of language for its own sake, and an understanding of its forms in all their diversity, then later study will be undermined. Particularly vital are the messages received by pupils in primary school about the worth of their own language and culture. In many Scottish primary schools, language differences are still left unexplored; the idea of language deficit – that the non-standard language of some pupils is linguistically defective – continues to be promoted, widely by implication, and in some places still by overt criticism.

In work for a final year dissertation, a BEd. student recently carried out a survey of the attitudes of pupils in the upper stages of an Ayrshire primary school towards Scottish language features in poetry and in speech (McLellan, 1993). The resulting snapshot was revealing, if depressing. Pupils were reluctant to approve of any non-standard dialect features, having imbibed an understanding that these are of low social value. They tolerated literary uses of dialect, but were not keen to use it in their own writing.

Studies by other students have given more cause for optimism, and have indicated what seem to be key elements in working with Scottish language and literature in the primary school.

Setting out to explore the supporting of pupils from speech to writing, one student began by actively engaging a class of upper primary pupils in examining their own spoken language (Miller, 1994). An overtly positive approach was taken by the student, helping the pupils to relish and enjoy the particular features of their dialect. Metalinguistic awareness was developed, and at the same time examples of dialect poetry were provided for discussion. The pupils in their own writing were encouraged to use features from their own dialect or from the texts they had discussed. The work stopped short of actually teaching Scottish language in a systematic way, since the focus was on attitudes. However, the freedom with which the pupils engaged in writing, in their 'true voices' as it were, and the positiveness they demonstrated towards Scottish language forms were remarkable.

In another study (Sloan, 1995), texts in Scottish dialects and standard English and discussion were used to help pupils to reflect upon aspects of Scottish history and culture. In order to set this reflection in a wider context, parallels were drawn between Scotland's past and world events which pupils were learning about through the mass media. For example, links were made between the Highland Clearances and the enforced movements of populations in Bosnia. This contextualisation of a historical and localised event in relation to a modern international situation appeared to help pupils to develop understandings and empathy. An added element was their very positive response towards the Scottish texts used in the study.

It is clear that there is nothing revolutionary about these pieces of work. Yet they all showed a firm grasp of good practice in the primary school, and, even more importantly, they showed awareness of the wider cultural and linguistic background within which Scottish literature, language and culture must be placed if our younger pupils are to make sense of them in their own lives. In the development of such work in primary schools, we are still in the phase of the enthusiasts. The number of teachers who wish to engage in work such as is described above is still small, though the work of people like Sheila Douglas and Liz Niven is making an impact. Materials for classroom use are at last beginning to emerge. The Scots Language Resource Centre in Perth has already produced materials for primary schools (SLRC, 1995), and will surely go on to be a clearing house of good works and good ideas.

However, the attitudes of teachers, and of Scottish society at large towards non-standard dialects and their use will have to be altered if Scottish language and literature are to move firmly into the mainstream of the curriculum. In the meantime, there are some pressing tasks to be undertaken:

1. the inclusion in the pre-service and in-service training of Scottish teachers of a grounding in linguistic concepts, exemplified in relation to Scottish language;

2. urgent discussions in Scottish schools, primary and secondary, that lead to clear policy formation in respect of the place of Scottish literature, language and culture in the curriculum;

3. continued production of Scottish texts and teaching materials;

4. sustained commitment by schools to do everything they can to give our pupils, through significant and pleasurable learning experiences, positive attitudes towards Scottish language and literature, which will help draw them towards wider understandings and fuller enjoyment.

The work has already begun.

REFERENCES

Liddell, G., 'Noo's no the oor fur cauld kale', *Laverock*, No. 1, 1995 published by ASLS.

Lorvik, M., *The Scottis Lass Betrayed* (Edinburgh: SCCC, 1995).

McLellan, L., unpublished action research study, 1993.

Miller, E., unpublished action research study, 1994.

SCCC, *Scottish Language: The Language Children Bring to School* (Edinburgh: SCCC, 1980).

SCCC, *The Kist/A' Chiste* (Edinburgh: SCCC/Nelson Blackie, 1996).

Sloan, S., unpublished action research study, 1995.

SOED, *National Guidelines: English Language 5-14* (Edinburgh: HMSO, 1991).

FURTHER READING

Douglas, S., *Scots in the 5–14 Courses: Starter Pack for Teachers* (Perth: Merlin Press, 1995).

Niven, L., *Scots Language 5–14* (Dumfries and Galloway Regional Council, 1995).

Scots Language Resource Centre, *Doadie's Boadie Scots Pack* (Perth: SLRC, 1995).

EXEMPLAR 37

Level/stage of school

P5/7; S1/2

Duration

Over two years as desired.

Topic and texts

Anthology and teaching materials: *The Kist/A' Chiste.*

Purposes

> To give pupils an extended experience of Scottish writing at an appropriate level in Scots, Gaelic and English.
>
> To give pupils opportunities for imaginative and useful language and literary work in the different modes of reading, writing, talk and listening over an extended period in the 9-14 stage.

Teaching approaches

As outlined in the extensive lesson materials accompanying the anthology, *The Kist.*

Products

> As suggested in the teaching materials.

Other Comments

The Kist is the most fully developed anthology and teaching pack of materials ever produced for schools in Scotland. Every school should have it among their resources. The producers of this volume regard it as indispensable for the effective promotion of Scottish literature and language in the upper primary and lower secondary schools. We include here, with permission, a full list of the contents of *The Kist*, so that teachers can judge its value for themselves.

> Aig Clachan Chalanais/At the Callanish Stones, *Iain Crichton Smith*
> The Fox's Skin, *Marion Angus*
> Hungry Waters, *Hugh MacDiarmid*
> Naebody, *Betty Allan*
> Breakin Rainbows, *Janet Paisley*
> Willie Wastle, *Robert Burns*
> The Nor'-Wast Men, *George Mackay Brown*
> The Toad, *Helen B. Cruickshank*
> Cearcail a' Chuain/Circle of Ocean, *Calum MacDonald*
> Grafitti, *Janet Paisley*
> Sunday Spectacular, *Ellie McDonald*

Wullie Waggletail, *William Soutar*
The Hen's Lament, *Sheena Blackhall*
Bairns, *Betty Allan*
Street Talk, *J. K. Annand*
Tinker, *J. K. Annand*
Crocodile, *J. K. Annand*
Heron, *J. K. Annand*
The Evacuee, *Jim Blaikie*
Seall Orms'/Look at Me, *Margaret Hulse*
The Fox without a Tail' *Robert Stephen*
The Ballad of Sawney Bean, *Lionel McClelland*
The Pouer o Advertisin, *William Neill*
A Dug A Dug, *Bill Keys*
The Jeery Piece Song, *Adam McNaughtan*
Lament for a Lost Dinner Ticket, *Margaret Hamilton*
Listen tae the Teacher, *Nancy Nicolson*
Colour Prejudice, *Doris Watt*
Cargoes, *Robert Johnson*
Oor Wullie, *Sunday Post*
Da Beltane Foy, *John J. Graham*
Beasties, *Helen J. Cruickshank*
Three Gleg Craiturs, *William J. Rae*
The Bubblyjock, *Hugh MacDiammid*
The Puddock, *J. M. Caie*
An Giomach/The Lobster, *Nicolson Institute School Magazine*
Doric-Reggae-Spider Rap, *Sheena Blackhall*
Thomas the Rhymer, *Anon.*
The Bogle, *W.D. Cocker*
Black Friday, *James Copeland*
The Wuid, *John Burns*
Iain agus na Drogaichean/Ian and the Drugs, *Myles M. Campbell*
The Christmas Story, *Pierowall Junior High School*
The Saubbath, *Robert McLellan*
The Coming of the Wee Malkies, *Stephen Muirine*
The Ballad of Janitor Mackay, *Margaret Green*
Fi'baw in the Street, *Robert Garioch*
The Auld Workin Collie, *Cecilia J. Mowatt*
Wur Cheeko, *Jenny S. Stewart*
A Christmas Poem, *Josephine Neill*
An Naoidhean/The Infant, *Finlay Madeod*
The Punnie, *Sheena Blackhall*
Shetlandic, *Rhoda Bulter*
The First Hoolit's Prayer, *Ian MacFadyen*
Owl, *Aonghas MacNeacail*
Brekken Beach, Nort Yell, *Christine De Luca*

Shetlan, *John Peterson*
In the Deid o Nicht, *Chris Morgan*
The Twa Corbies, *Anon.*
Said the Mole, *Aonghas MacNeacail*
Da Selkie, *Rhoda Bulter*
Catching the Salmon, *Neil Gunn*
Kiniochbervie, *John Bellany*
A Pan Drop Man, *Raymond Vettese*
Air Mointeach Shuardail/On Swordale Moor, *Derick Thomson*
A' Bhideo/The Video, *Alasdair Campbell*
Bessie Dunlop, *John Hodgart*
North-East Nineties Rap, *Sheena Blackhall*
Black Andie's Tale of Tod Lapraik, *Robert Louis Stevenson*
Na Lochlannaich A' Tighinn Air Tir An Nis/The Norsemen Coming
Ashore at Ness, *Derick Thomson*
From 'Unrelated Incidents', – No. 3, *Tom Leonard*
See You?, *Donald Campbell*
A Scottish Hoy-you, *Hugh McMillan*
Highlander: Free Fall Videocassette sleeve
Fill-iu Oro Hu O, *Traditional waulking song*
Answermachine, *W. N. Herbert*
Sharleen: Ah'm Shy, *Janet Paisley*
The First Date, *Sandra Savage*
The Broons, *Sunday Post*
The Peerie Grandson, *C. P.Costie*
Dithis/Two People, *A. Smith*
Shankie's Tale, *Stanley Robertson*
The Wee Magic Stane, *John McEvoy*
Sir Patrick Spens, *Anon.*
'S Dia Mor Gar Beannachadh/May Great God Bless Us, *Anon.*
Twenty-third Psalm, Shepherd's Version, *Catherine Harvey*
Empty Vessel, *Hugh MacDianmid*
Cragsman's Widow, *Robert Rendall*
A Hind's Daughter, *Sir James Guthrie*
Clach an Truiseal/The Trushal Stone, *C. MacLeod*
The Poacher to Orion, *Violet Jacob*
Gin I Was God, *Charles Murray*
Crowdieknowe, *Hugh MacDiarmid*
Mansie's Threshing, *Robert Rendall*
Scotland, *George Ritchie*
Da Diary o Gideon Hunter, *Peter Ratter*
Lockerb8e Elegy, *William Hershaw*
Cairteal gu Meadhan-Latha/A Quarter to Midday, *Angus Peter Campbell*
The Bonnie Broukit Bairn, *Hugh MacDiarmid*

EXEMPLAR 38

Level/stage of school

P 6/7 or S 1/2.

Duration

2 periods.

Topic/text(s)

A Scots A-Z (an illustrated alphabet).

Purposes

To increase pupils' awareness and knowledge of Scots vocabulary in its range and expressiveness.

To give practice in the use of Scots dictionaries and wordbooks.

Teaching approaches

1. Divide the class into groups of 3-4 pupils, and give each group a copy of the *Pocket Scots Dictionary*, paper for writing and illustrating, and copies of old magazines and colour supplements.

2. Using the dictionaries, pupils select Scots words to illustrate the alphabet, one for each letter, one alphabet per group.

3. Pupils prepare a sheet for each letter, with letter (illuminated or decorated as desired) followed by word and illustration.

4. Alphabets (A-Zs) are gathered together in books for display and circulation.

Products

Group A-Z Books.

Supporting Materials

Copies of *Pocket Scots Dictionary*.

One copy each of *Concise Scots Dictionary* and *Scots Thesaurus*.

Other Comments

Only one of many ways to develop awareness of Scots language by pupils.

EXEMPLAR 39

Level/stage of school

S1

Duration

4 periods.

Topics/text(s)

Linguistic autobiography.

Purposes

To make pupils aware of the different languages which are or have been spoken in their families.

To encourage pupils to see bilingualism in a positive light.

To help pupils feel that all languages have equal validity.

To encourage discussion between pupils and their families, involving parents/grandparents in the pupils' schoolwork.

Teaching approaches

1. Discuss with the class the idea that different languages are often spoken within families, and that as families move from one country or area to another, languages can change or even be lost. Reference can be made to

Scots and Gaelic within Scotland, and other languages like Urdu, Chinese, etc. Pupils can be issued with a questionnaire to discuss with parents and grandparents or other older family members for homework; they find out which areas or countries family members have come from, why they moved, which languages are or have been spoken within the family, and what attitudes they have to language use or change.

2. Pupils report back to class or group. On maps of the world, Britain or Scotland as appropriate, a picture of the class origins is built up with pins or markers. An accompanying wall display is built up, presenting information about class members, with photos of themselves and families. The teacher should also provide personal information.

3. Pupils can then make labels for objects in classroom, greetings and messages for the wall display in all the different languages mentioned. A multiple-language dictionary of common words and phrases can also be made, entailing use of dictionaries. Translations of notices around the school into different languages can also be made for public display. Scots and Gaelic versions should certainly be included. By the end of the work, all pupils will have had exposure to a variety of languages and should be aware of the validity of them all.

Products

Wall displays.

Notices.

Class dictionary.

Pupil language notebooks.

Supporting materials

Dictionaries of different languages (including Scots and Gaelic dictionaries).

Cardboard and display materials.

Maps.

Other comments

Pupils can define 'family' in the way most appropriate to themselves. Clearly, the more extended the family the better. Short-distance movement within a city or district can easily be accommodated within the work.

EXEMPLAR 40

Level/stage of school

S2

Duration

4 periods.

Topic/text(s)

A study of 'Tam o' Shanter' by Robert Burns.

Purposes

> To introduce pupils to a powerful, vivid and imaginative story and help them to enjoy it fully.

> To encourage pupils to express their own imaginative ideas in a variety of ways.

Teaching approaches

1. Discuss with pupils how superstitions about witches and ghosts have survived through the centuries and how legends and folktales used to be transmitted orally from one generation to another. Refer to Hallowe'en, to stories about the Devil, to the current popularity of supernatural horror stories. Bring in the idea of making jokes about the supernatural to keep fears at bay.

2. Listen to a good rendering of 'Tam o' Shanter' on tape or video; have copies for pupils to refer to. Discuss how the story has different scenes like a film. What would be the main elements in each scene? Pupils could discuss how Burns gives information about each scene in the words of the poem. Focus on certain episodes for groups to discuss and do some writing, for example the whole diatribe of Kate against Tam's drinking habits; the full stories behind the references to the smothered chapman, the death of drunken Charlie, the murdered bairn, the suicide of Mungo's mother; how Nannie had become one of the local witches; reports in the local paper about strange goings-on at Alloway Kirk; Tam's explanation to Kate of what had happened to him and her reactions.

3. Collect all the writing into either a wall display with illustrations or a folder giving 'The Full Story of Tam o' Shanter's Meeting with the Witches', interweaving the pupils' writings with the text of the poem.

Products

As indicated above.

Supporting materials

Stimulus material in pictures or writing about witches, the Devil and the supernatural.

Other comments

This treatment of 'Tam o' Shanter' is aimed at younger pupils. However, like the ballads, the poem can be enjoyed and studied on several different levels. Another exemplar deals with 'Tam o' Shanter' at a level suitable for senior pupils.

10

———— • ————

IDENTITY, CULTURE AND LITERATURE: SCOTTISH LANGUAGE AND LITERATURE IN THE MIDDLE STAGES

David Drever

Before poking about in the dusty and dog-eared file labelled 'Standard Grade', it is worthwhile restating a central tenet of this book. Scottish Literature and the languages of Scotland are at the heart of present-day Scottish culture. The historical and contemporary evidence of this project make that statement a truism, notwithstanding the myriad definitions available of 'culture'. However, in view of the inclusive demands of school education, it is as well to leave the term 'Scottish culture' on the broadest canvas possible.

Perhaps not so self-evident is the growing sense of Scottishness that is now prevalent. Today there are more images of Scotland and a wider range of Scottish identities available than at any time of recent history. In the political sphere a degree of autonomy and control is an imminent reality in the form of a Scottish Parliament – the implications of this for cultural agencies, including education, are profound. In the sphere of popular culture – television, rock music, films – there has been an upsurge of interest that has its origin in the specific cultural identities being espoused. In a similar way, much of the current interest in Scottish writing derives from its specific cultural provenance and its authentic linguistic expression.

Paradoxically this growing sense of cultural identity has been accompanied by a realisation that there are, in fact, a range of identities – defined by gender, geography, class, religion, language – that are inclusive parts of being Scottish. This perception challenges the corrosive caricature of Scottishness that was self-conscious, partial and didactic. Our contemporary cultural identities are given confidence and authenticity by being rooted in real places and real lives.

Scottish literature has a central place within any consideration of Scottish culture and identity. In historical and contemporary terms it has given emotional, intellectual and artistic expression to the experience of being Scottish. In a related way, the actual spoken and written languages of our people have been an existing and true expression of these cultural identities.

The aims and objectives of English teachers can be located easily within this context: personal, social and intellectual growth through the experience of literature and language (in their broadest senses) lies at the heart of English teaching. The task is to place the resources of Scottish literature and the languages of Scotland within the curricular and pedagogic reach of teachers and, accordingly, their pupils. Standard Grade English has a particular role in this process.

STANDARD GRADE WITHIN THE BIGGER PICTURE

There is perhaps one more observation to be made before dusting down the Standard Grade file. It is common practice to address the three stages – Lower, Middle and Upper School – discretely. This is not surprising: S4 Standard Grade and S5/6 Higher/Sixth Year Studies. have traditionally been subject to quite different assessment regulations from the Scottish Examination Board (SEB) and SCOTVEC; in recent times there have been weak attempts to tack a system of National Tests in S1 and S2 onto the 5–14 Programme. This separation of the three stages has often been accompanied by different types of class grouping within each stage – mixed ability in S1/2; setting into Credit/General and General/Foundation in S3/4; Higher and Module classes in S5/6.

These factors, taken alongside the traditional target stages of curriculum development, encourage a pigeonholing mentality that in fact runs counter to the daily experience of classroom teaching. In the secondary school the processes of teaching and learning are being seen increasingly as part of a continuum stretching from S1 to S6.

This notion of a 'seamless garment' is an important one for Scottish literature and language. The use of Scottish literature in the curriculum should be natural and pervasive: an annual orgy of Burns in January for a few classes only serves to marginalise pupils' perceptions of Scottish literature. Rather we need an understanding that Scottish literature will be at home in any year group, in any classroom, and will be accessible to any pupil. This understanding will develop to the extent that teachers have appropriate Scottish texts and support materials from which they can select according to the needs of their pupils.

PAST AND PRESENT PRONOUNCEMENTS

Standard Grade is the most settled stage in the English curriculum. Whereas guidance on S1 and S2 in the 5–14 Programme was published in 1991, and Higher Still is ongoing at the date of writing, formal advice on Standard Grade from the Scottish Examination Board dates from the *Revised Arrangements* document of 1987, although most of it belongs properly to its first publication in 1984.

A comparison of the Standard Grade advice and the later pronouncements on 5–14 and Higher Still reveals the formal progress that has been made on the place of Scottish literature and language. The 5–14 document addresses the issue of Scottish culture and situates a discussion of the spoken dialects of Scotland within that, making the link between language and identity. Encouragement for the wide use of Scottish texts of all kinds is given. In Higher Still it is probable that there will be a specific Scottish textual option within some courses. In contrast, the Standard Grade advice is distinguished by its paucity of comment on Scottish literature and language.

The *Revised Arrangements* advice of 1987 sets general aims and addresses the purposes of an English course in terms of pupils' personal and social growth and the development of language skills. Such a course:

> should make them aware of the main ways in which language works in their lives. Within this context, pupils should be made aware of the cultural diversity in Scotland and of the contribution of minority cultures. (SEB, 1987, p. 4)

This statement is an important affirmation of multicultural Scotland and the contribution of ethnic minority cultures within that. However, it fails to address the central question of Scottish culture and pupils' experience of it. The validity of minority cultures is quite rightly asserted, yet the equally valid historic culture of Scotland, and its identity as expressed in language and literature is ignored.

A following paragraph concludes with little enthusiasm:

> If Scottish pupils are to achieve the linked aims of linguistic development and personal enrichment described above, it is important that they should have some experience of the work of Scottish writers. (SEB, 1987, p. 4)

Later in the *Arrangements* document, under the heading of the skill area Talking, there is advice on language use:

> It is also desirable that pupils should be introduced to some of the main ways in which language varies: Scottish forms of English, regional dialects, standard and non-standard forms ...

This leaves much unsaid. Standard Grade was the first time that the skill area of Talking had been rated highly enough to merit Scottish Examination Board assessment – it was allocated 33 per cent of the final award, and a strong case was advanced for its importance in the cognitive and social development of pupils. Yet there is silence on the vexed question of dialect versus Standard English forms and the validity of pupils' own use of dialect in talk activities. These are issues that English teachers have long fought over. No doubt that fight will continue – but here was an opportunity to put it within an informed framework that would have recognised the importance of pupils' own identity and dialect.

The final reference in the *Arrangements* document deals with the use of Scottish materials:

> Although a Scottish dimension will not be mandatory in the Standard Grade course, Scottish materials may be used in assessment in the following ways.
>
> The external test of Reading will frequently, though not invariably, make some use of texts by Scottish writers. These texts may occasionally include Scots language forms.
>
> It is open to the candidate in compiling the folio of coursework on Reading to submit one, two or all three pieces of extended writing on literary/media texts of Scottish origin.

The overall impression from the 1987 *Revised Arrangements* in Standard Grade English is one of acknowledgement rather than positive promotion of Scottish literature.

THE CURRENT POSITION

However, teachers find themselves in quite different circumstances a decade on from the introduction of Standard Grade. Reference has already been made to progress in S1/2 and S5/6. In addition to guidance and encouragement from SOEID and SEB, there has been a developing trend for teachers to select Scottish texts for study. This has been most obvious at the Higher stage, where the inclusion of major Scottish texts in the Set Text option has confirmed teachers' growing confidence in this area. It is interesting to see the SEB noting the proliferation of Scottish texts in Certificate of Sixth Year Studies dissertations in the 1995 diet of exams (*Draft Report of the Scottish Exam Board*, February 1996). It may well be that the increased exposure to Scottish literature in S5 is leading students' own preferences in the elective areas in Sixth Year Studies.

Standard Grade lacks the benefits of either the guidance of the 5–14 English language programme or the syllabus and assessment – led directives of Higher Still. However, S3/4 has advantages in being the most settled curricular level. Teachers have long experience of the required breadth and balance within the Standard Grade curriculum – and these issues tend to be a regular and lively source of anxiety to teachers when developing new curricula. There is a similar familiarity with the needs of Standard Grade English assessment. Overall there is probably a sense of security and confidence in teaching this stage of English that can benefit from an increasing awareness of the importance of Scottish literature.

An important caveat to this observation would be a caution against creating a vacuum in the middle years, as the innovations of the lower and upper school suggests the use of texts and materials that would happily prosper in S3 and S4. For reasons already suggested, the teaching of Scottish literature has been most prevalent in the upper school. A continuing relegation will only be damaging: it will marginalise the texts and materials; more importantly it will create perceptions about Scottish literature, language and culture that are narrow and elitist.

Far more effective is to see Standard Grade Scottish literature on the continuum: a progression from 5–14, and a building block of Higher Still.

TEACHING SCOTTISH LITERATURE AT STANDARD GRADE

A starting point is the earlier observation that teachers are experienced and secure in their teaching at Standard Grade. Most have developed well tried strategies and methodologies for teaching the four skill areas of Reading, Writing, Talking and Listening. It is a manifest cliché that no two teachers teach in the same way; indeed there are as many successful strategies for good teaching as there are good teachers. The same methods and strategies are applicable to the teaching of Scottish texts; there is no qualitative difference in how we teach them, and there is certainly no correct blueprint available.

However, the cultural context of pupils and teachers in Scottish schools does have an important bearing on how the teaching of Scottish literature can have an enriching and liberating effect on pupils. For example, by exploring their own dialects, pupils can be shown that their own language is an important and legitimate means of communicating in imaginative, intellectual and emotional terms. The starting point is the articulation of pupils' own identity and experiences – a fruitful exercise for adolescents at their stage of maturity. From this specific and probably local language use, pupils can be introduced to the concepts of the variety, mutability and validity of all dialects. Further exploration can then be made of written and literary uses of dialect and other expressive forms of Scottish language.

Similarly, there are a wealth of Scottish texts that establish relevance between pupils' worlds and that which lies beyond their own experience. Often our pupils share a common cultural experience with these texts that is not realised or not acknowledged. An important part of teaching is to tease out and establish that link. That might well mean developing a historical context for reading Scottish texts that allows pupils to reflect upon past and present experiences of being Scottish.

Standard Grade assessment needs are already well satisfied by Scottish texts. There is scope for Critical Responses using Scottish texts in all the genres of the Reading Folio: Prose, including non-fiction; Poetry; Drama; Media – recent successes of Scottish film-makers or films with Scottish subjects are now stimulating interest. The Expressive element in the Writing Folio, and the Imaginative Response to literary text(s) in the Reading Folio, both offer the possibility of an extended use of Scots dialect, as does the Writing Paper in the final exam.

The use of Scots is not proscribed in any of the Standard Grade arrangements that relate to Talk and its assessment. By analogy, if Scottish texts are as valid in the curriculum as English texts, then Scots language forms can be equally appropriate in Talk activities, including the assessment of Discussion and Individual Talk. While there is probably little formal assessment of Talk activities conducted in Scots, much informally assessed Talk in the shape of class and group discussion takes place in discourses full of dialect use.

TEACHERS AS LEARNERS

There is a widespread – but fertile! – ignorance among English teachers of the richness of Scottish material. The reasons for this are rooted in our culture itself and the place of Scottish education within that. There is also the mundane but vital issue of the availability of both primary texts and support materials. This series addresses both these issues in a comprehensive way, and is part of a trend in publishing that is simultaneously foregrounding the wealth of Scottish literature and the practical application of it in schools and universities.

Where teachers are developing new skills and exploring new territory, there is a need for an approach that favours humility and cooperation. It is a tribute to the professional skills of English teachers that they subvert, as a matter of course, new support materials and commercially produced teaching packs to their own specific needs. Collaborative work and shared perceptions within English departments, and where possible at Authority level, will deepen teachers' understanding of Scottish literature and language, and will sponsor an enthusiasm for it that will grip the hearts and minds of our pupils.

BIBLIOGRAPHY

SEB, *Revised Arrangements in Standard Grade English* (Scottish Examination Board, 1987).
SEB, *Report of the Scottish Examination Board to 31 December 1995* (Scottish Examination Board, 1996).

EXEMPLAR 41

Level/stage of school

S3/4.

Duration

2 periods.

Topic/text(s)

Poem: 'Lament for the Makaris' by William Dunbar.

Purposes

To let pupils hear a good reading of the poem that brings out the flavour of the language and the mood of the poet.

To familiarise pupils with Dunbar's poem, its language and ideas, by means of group work aimed at building up a photo-album illustrating the progress of the poem.

Teaching approaches

1. Supply pupils with copies of the poem. Play an audio-cassette reading of the poem for pupils to follow from their texts. Discuss points from the poem that arise from this activity.

2. Divide the pupils into pairs or threes for cooperative work; allocate two consecutive stanzas to each pair for discussion and illustration with selected photos from magazines. Pupils agree on the best pictures to illustrate the images and ideas of their stanzas.

3. Pupils mount pictures on sheets along with the relevant lines of the poem. The sheets are then assembled to give the complete poem with illustrations, and are then bound together and titled.

4. Follow-up discussion of the poem as a whole, and appropriate writing on the theme, e.g. a modern prose version with contemporary references.

Products

The completed class photo-album of the poem.

Relevant writing as follow-up to the work on the poem.

Supporting materials

Copies of the poem.

Audio-tape with reading of the poem (Scotsoun Cassettes SSC 020: poem read by Robert Garioch).

Old copies of general interest magazines and colour supplements.

Concise Scots Dictionary.

Other comments

This poem lends itself well to this treatment because of its 'catalogue' format. The technique can be applied to any appropriate poem, of whatever period.

EXEMPLAR 42

Level/stage of school

S3/4.

Duration

2 or 3 periods.

Topic/text(s)

The ballad: 'Lamkin', Anon.

Purposes

To study a traditional ballad, using the story structure as the focus for work.

Teaching approaches

1. Supply pupils with copies of the ballad. Read the ballad aloud either in one reading followed by discussion, or in sections with discussion after each.

2. Pupils in groups discuss how to divide the ballad into scenes for possible film or dramatic presentation. Pupils then prepare storyboards of the action with brief descriptions of each scene (location, characters, action, mood). Pupils discuss what 'missing' scenes might have to be written into the action.

3. General discussion of group conclusions, followed by appropriate writing (review of television play of ballad, instructions to cameraman for one major scene, the speech of Lamkin's defence counsel at his trial, etc.).

Products

> Storyboards in folders from groups.
>
> Appropriate follow-up creative writing.
>
> Essay on the question of ballad as literature

Supporting materials

> Copies of ballad, with glossary of words.

Other comments

If the class and the teacher have experience of dramatic work in the classroom (or in a studio), a suitable end-product might be a dramatisation of the ballad. Dialogue for scenes can be improvised in groups; a few basic props will suffice. Many ballads lend themselves to dramatic work, and the necessary discussion of how to stage it will involve grappling with any obscurities of the text and fleshing out the bare ballad narrative.

EXEMPLAR 43

Level/stage of school

S3/4.

Duration

2 periods.

Topic/text(s)

A mock elegy: 'Elegy on Maggy Johnston', by Allan Ramsay.

Purposes

> To study a Scots poem by a major forerunner of Robert Burns.
>
> To examine how a poem can have both an apparent purpose and a real underlying purpose that may be at odds with each other.

Teaching approaches

1. Supply copies of the poem to pupils and read it (or listen to a taped reading). Discuss the apparent purpose, the lament for the death of Maggy Johnston, and consider how it seems to be unsatisfactory or inadequate in this respect. What elements seem to be lacking?

2. Discuss with pupils (or have pupils discuss in groups) what the poem is really about. Is it a celebration of social drinking, going out on the town with the intention of getting drunk? Note that this poem was written by Ramsay as a young man for the literary/social Easy Club to which he belonged in Edinburgh. Does this change our feelings about the poem? Is it a poem that fits our modern sensibilities?

3. Look at the uses of Scots language: the vivid but now obscure vocabulary (a glossary should be available, and notes on some of the difficult references); the mixture of Scots with the elegant Augustan diction of the opening, like an elegy by Pope or a fashionable English writer. What is Ramsay up to? Is he suggesting something about the social purposes of Scots and English, or making some kind of language statement?

4. The work might conclude with some writing, for example an obituary on Maggy Johnston for the Edinburgh papers, a letter attacking or support-ing the poem's attitudes to drinking and drunkenness.

Products

Pupils' annotated copies and notes.

Writings by pupils (obituaries, letters, etc.).

Supporting materials

Concise Scots Dictionary.

Glossary and notes on poem (to be found in *Selected Poems of Ramsay and Fergusson.*

Examples of newspaper obituaries and letters.

Other comments

Note how the epitaph of the poem echoes that on Ben Jonson the dramatist: 'O rare Ben Jonson'. One of Ramsay's interests was the theatre and drama.

EXEMPLAR 44

Level/stage of school

S3/4.

Duration

2/3 periods.

Topic/text(s)

Short story, 'Peggy's Walk', by Pat Gerber: a woman's voice in Scots.

Purposes

To read and study a short story dealing with a topical social issue (ageing and Alzheimer's disease).

To examine a text with a woman's voice in Scots carrying the narrative.

Teaching approaches

1. Read the story with the class, bringing out the shifting nature of the narrative voice, moving imperceptibly from a neutral narrative voice into Peggy's Glasgow voice and back.

2. Discuss the story, identifying the sections where Peggy has lost touch with the current world around her.

3. Discuss how the city is presented as an unfriendly dangerous place for Peggy now, compared with how she knew it in the past.

4. Raise, if it has not already come up, the topic of Alzheimer's disease and the current awareness of it in society. Apply it to the account of Peggy's nocturnal excursion.

5. Finish the discussion with a look at the language of the story and how Peggy's voice expressing her viewpoint fluctuates with a more English narrative voice observing her from outside. How effective is this as a narrative style?

6. Possible follow-up writing might take the topic of Peggy's daughter Angela and her feelings as she goes to Peggy's flat to collect some clothes

for her mother in hospital. What would her voice be like? Would she feel any responsibility for what has happened?

Products

Pupils' notes on the story.

Pupils' creative writing to follow up the reading.

Supporting material

Information material on the needs and care of the elderly and on Alzheimer's disease.

Other comments

Maiden Voyage by Pat Gerber contains a number of stories and prose pieces suitable for reading by pupils at the Standard Grade stage.

EXEMPLAR 45

Level/stage at school

S3/4.

Duration

3 periods.

Topic/text(s)

Long short story: 'The Bottle Imp', by R. L. Stevenson.

Purposes

To read and study a short story by one of the classic writers of Scottish literature which comes out of experience and observation of a way of life remote from Scotland.

To observe traditional themes within an exotic fictional setting.

To predict the outcome of a developing story from clues of context and experience of other stories.

Teaching approaches

1. Supply the story to pupils in sections and read it in stages, discussing the progress of the story after each section and trying to predict how it will develop beyond each stopping point.

2. Suggested sections are:
   (a) the first buying of the bottle by Keawe ('...afraid of that bottle');
   (b) the selling of the bottle to Lopaka ('...escaped out of that trouble');
   (c) Keawe's life of prosperity ('...I was so pleased to be rid of');
   (d) the second buying of the bottle by Keawe ('...darkness fell upon the light');
   (e) Keawe and Kokua try to sell the bottle ('...be it mine to perish');
   (f) Kokua's buying of the bottle ('...fell in a deep slumber instantly');
   (g) the final sale of the bottle (to the end).

3. The reading and discussion of the story will take more than one period, since there may be many clues of context to discuss, as well as the pupils' expectations of how such a story ought to turn out.

4. Other discussion points for later consideration are: the world and time of the story (the Pacific, the nineteenth century, the sense of an older, superstitious society being changed by Christianity and European and American values); the well-known story of the genie in the bottle who grants wishes transferred from the Arabian Nights stories to a new setting.

Products

Pupils' notes on the story.

Follow-up writing (e.g. the experience of one of the other owners of the bottle).

Other comments

Some background information on R. L. Stevenson, his life and writing, and how he came to settle in the Pacific so far away from Scotland, might be of interest to pupils.

11

———— • ————

RE-READING SCOTTISH LITERATURE: CRITICAL ISSUES IN THE UPPER SECONDARY STAGES

James McGonigal

A Scottish English teacher: the tensions implicit in that oddly lopsided title have become ever more apparent since I began teaching in 1970. Sometimes the strains are socio-linguistic (most Scottish teachers can speak, or at least comprehend, a version of English radically different from the standard form it is their job to teach) and sometimes they are political, but more often than not the tensions centre on the nature of the subject and the way it is taught, or might be taught. Matters become even more complex when post–16 school pupils become 'students' who are attaining some independence of mind or action, together with a growing awareness of their own ancestry and culture. Scottish language and literature, opened up for them in these upper stages of the second-ary school, can become a useful debatable land where some at least of the cultural tensions implicit in teaching and learning English in Scot-land can be admitted and explored.

The most recent report on the teaching of English in Scottish secondary schools (SOED, 1992) deliberately foregrounds the Scottish dimension of the English teacher's work. Beginning with John Galt's reference in *The Seamstress* (1833) to 'the fortunate circumstance of the Scotch possessing the whole range of the English language as well as their own', its opening paragraph goes on to affirm that 'Scottish English and Scots are now ... rightly recognised as significant and distinctive varieties of language, with their own continuing history and literature.' Such distinctiveness of language is also clearly echoed in Scottish educational structures: we have the more broadly based Higher Grade (combined sometimes with separate modules in communication and literature for less confident students) and the Certificate of Sixth Year Studies at ages 17 and 18, for instance, rather than the 'gold standard' of the A level south of the border. It is a more open question, however, to what extent such distinctiveness also operates within the curriculum of English or in the methodologies encountered by senior pupils in most Scottish classrooms.

Yet it is at this S5/6 stage that the Scottish dimension of English teaching is most open to examination, in several senses. There is, first of all, the most obvious sense in which specified or set texts for study at both Higher and Sixth Year Studies levels have always included a range of Scottish authors which may direct teaching and learning towards (at the time of writing) Burns, Crichton Smith, Rona Munro and Grassic Gibbon at Higher Grade, or towards Bridie, Henryson, the Ballads, Morgan, Scott, Galt, Gunn, Lindsay, McGrath, Lochhead, Hogg, Jenkins, Spark, Stevenson, Douglas Brown, McIlvanney or Mackay Brown at Sixth Year Studies. As these specified works are gradually altered over time, purchased sets of such Scottish texts remain viable for use with other year groups or, more likely, as a valid focus for general literary study and assessment, or as focus texts for more independent study towards the Review of Personal Reading (some 1,500 words in length) which forms part of the Personal Studies Folio at Higher, or the dissertation at Sixth Year Studies (between 3,000 and 4,000 words in length). In a recent indicative survey of Folio authors and texts (McGonigal, 1997), there does appear to be some indication of such 'assessment-led' development of a distinctively Scottish literary curriculum at the upper stages.

Language study arises naturally enough in the context of such reading, and also in the need to prepare students to become more sensitive to the linguistic dimensions of Scottish texts chosen for close reading. It is at this stage of more demanding texts and reading strategies that teachers can reveal the depth of their own literary and linguistic awareness, holding up for examination at a fairly sophisticated level such issues as identity, motivation and consequence, theme, style and form. At the same time, they often find themselves responding to the differing interpretations or insights offered by intelligent younger readers who are encountering such texts probably for the first time and certainly from a different viewpoint. Given the diversity of dialect and social frameworks in contemporary Scotland, the Scottish text and context will always complicate this process in challenging ways.

In the late 1970s in Lockerbie, for example, I remember teaching Iain Crichton Smith's *Consider the Lilies* to a 'repeat Higher' set of mainly S6 and some S5 pupils. They found themselves moved and engaged by the plight of the Gaelic populace cruelly displaced by sheep and Sassenach shepherds and lawyers. I suggested that their own great-great-grandfathers might easily have been among those very shepherds, Dumfriesshire being good sheep-rearing country and having itself suffered from the displacement of farmworkers through enclosure just before the Highlands did (Richards, 1982, pp. 186–90). There was dismay or doubt about this laying bare of local complicity, and I was uneasily aware of the partial and shallow nature of all of our knowledge of Scottish history. I failed to pursue the difference which this new knowledge might make to us as readers; to a great extent it seemed that the divide between the Gaelic and Lowland worlds still operated. In any case, no question in the Higher English Literature paper then would invite or welcome an ideological response.

Such memories, personal as they are, suggest some interesting developments over the succeeding twenty-year period. *Consider the Lilies* was at that point our main Scottish text, although the new Head of English, an Aberdeenshire man, would shortly introduce Gunn and Mackay Brown. Since then, teachers have been enabled to move away from an almost exclusively English canon of texts (whether traditional or modern: Austen and Dickens replaced by Orwell and Golding) and to begin to explore with their pupils a Scottish dimension, often regional and mainly twentieth-century texts, with north-east and west coast writers predominant.

Their critical treatment has remained largely 'traditional', however. Using Scottish texts for Higher study, many teachers will normally employ the New Critical/Leavisite approach in which they were originally trained, seeking an inherent textual unity or authenticity, the very existence of which contemporary critics might well now question. This may be due to the sort of insecurity with the social and political ramifications of Scottish texts recounted above; it must also partly be due to the necessarily general and basic spadework of explication demanded by a Scottish literature being rescued from neglect, and made available in such works as *Ten Modern Scottish Novels* (1984) by Murray and Tait, or *Modern Scottish Literature* (1983) by Alan Bold, or the useful Scotnotes and Commentary Cassettes on key texts and authors which have been commissioned by the Schools Committee of the Association for Scottish Literary Studies throughout the 1980s and 1990s. These were written for an intended readership of teachers and fifth- and sixth-year pupils by scholars or creative writers, or those such as Iain Crichton Smith, Edwin Morgan or Roderick Watson who have managed to be both.

Such basic critical apparatus followed on from a vital creative period in the 1970s, when Morgan, Crichton Smith and Mackay Brown in particular revealed a new maturity and confidence among Scotland's post-Renaissance poets. Younger, edgier, urban voices such as those of Leonard or Lochhead had also begun to catch the ear of university students of literature and language, who became teachers in their turn and communicated this enthusiasm to pupils. A growing number of these younger teachers also began to possess degree passes in the more theoretical English and cultural studies of the period, as well as in Scottish literature, and sought to pass on the redefinition of a national literature which such studies were shaping. Since they taught to some extent against the grain of a largely 1960s liberal curriculum of mainly modern English (male) writers, there was often in their teaching an effective proselytising enthusiasm which affected both pupils and colleagues.

Meanwhile, the development of Standard Grade English with its new focus on talk and listening brought re-examination of accent, dialect, standard and non-standard language and a more sophisticated awareness of the socio-linguistic contexts of these. Group talk meant that dialect was more frequently heard and, in some sense, officially sanctioned in the classroom, a matter of discussion or negotiation itself rather than of simple prohibition. Admittedly there was (and remains) continued insecurity among some teachers and communities in general about the shifting boundaries between dialect, slang and informality, especially where urban demotic speech figures in literary works.

These boundaries are social but also ideological, and when Higher Grade courses and examinations were revised in the late 1980s, there was a recognition in its Rationale of the importance of senior pupils becoming more acutely aware 'of forms of language which are fleeting in their manifestations but powerful in their influence: the visual and auditory codes of the mass media and their own and others' speech. Such growing awareness and understanding must be complemented by increasing sharpness in powers of discrimination, debate and analysis' (SEB, 1991, p. 4). The raw material for such analysis and discrimination existed most obviously in the local language of home and community but also in the Scottish texts they studied: here the interweaving of spoken or written speech, of direct dialect speech with authorial standard voices, could most easily be observed and considered.

Key understandings for this sort of activity at Higher include familiarity with 'register, Scots language forms, regional and other dialects, standard and non-standard forms and multi-cultural varieties' and also with the ways in which 'the vocabulary, pronunciation and structures of language change over time' (SEB, 1991, para. 1.4). Here Scottish literature in all its regional and historical variety offers a coherent means of holding up for examination the subtle and sometimes vexed contexts of language variety in Scottish society past and present. All teachers of English will recognise how 'chauvinistic' pupils can appear about varieties of Scottish dialect and accent other than their own, while accepting with relative openness other varieties of English encountered in, say, North American, West Indian or South African writing. It seems almost as if lack of a national political definition has driven such distinctions inward, creating quite strict 'parochial' boundaries at a psychological level, rather than an ability to view such differences as subtly varied and historical markers of one people.

Whatever the root of the matter, the introduction of independent study in the Review of Personal Reading has allowed Scottish texts from different regions to be further explored by students whose attention has been caught by teacher enthusiasm or by the inherent qualities of particular Scottish writers. And the increase in the range of Scottish authors within the Specified Texts has meant that, despite some teacher resistance to the perceived narrowing of their professional autonomy in choice of texts for study (which in reality had become in many schools a fairly narrow and derivative canon of mainstream twentieth-century English authors) there was a generation of young Scots who had been exposed to more poetry by Burns or MacCaig, for example, than had been the case for decades: many of these young people could respond with genuine sadness to the latter's death in January 1996, and with informed recognition to the former's bicentennial revival in the same month.

How are Scottish texts to be handled in the upper school? Recommended activities in the Revised Higher course include identification of 'the main concerns, structures and styles of text and, where appropriate, inter-relationships between texts'. These are too obvious to need rehearsal here. But there is also a need to acquire 'awareness of the contexts (literary, historical, ideological) of a text' and to apply 'a knowledge of literary concepts and critical approaches' (SEB, 1991, para. 1.1) and it may be useful to consider briefly the impact on the study of Scottish texts of some of the newer, more theoretical ways of reading to which younger teachers have been exposed at university. 'Exposed': there is an intriguing sense of risk or disclosure inherent in that word, which may signal a way to reinvigorate the life of a text made tame by repeated exposition.

What would such a new approach to reading Scottish texts actually look like? Perhaps we can keep as a constant among the swirling clouds of critical theory the novel mentioned earlier, *Consider the Lilies*, and examine it from different perspectives. This may illustrate not only the different directions in which literary criticism has gone over the last forty to fifty years, but also suggest those in which classroom teaching might validly follow. Murray and Tait express some surprise in their

Ten Scottish Novels (1984) that whole areas of Scotland's history such as the Reformation and later Disruption of the Church or twentieth-century working-class political struggles remain largely untapped by the novels they study, but that the Highland Clearances are frequently used 'to epitomise pain and protest at deracination and division' (p. 4) not only in *Consider the Lilies* but in Gunn's *Butcher's Broom* and *The Silver Darlings*, MacColla's *And the Cock Crew* and, a modern parallel, in Mackay Brown's *Greenvoe*. An approach through the archetypal criticism developed in the 1940s and 1950s, with its emphasis on mythical patterns in texts might suggest why that should be so.

The teacher as archetypal reader might explore this myth of severance in *Consider the Lilies*, and the ways in which Mrs Scott's separation from love and spontaneity mirrors various other cultural banishments: a sternly Calvinistic view of fallen humanity; the separation of religion from life and church from people in an ironic negation of the 'pastor's' role; the pattern of the rebel hero in the mason, Donald Macleod, who finally at least to some extent redeems her self-distancing from husband and son; or the scapegoating function of gossip in a small community, paralleling a more insidious racial scapegoating of Highland people by Southern powers. Beneath the plot we may discern biblical archetypes of spiritual loss, but also of the redemptive power which arises from challenging an established religion which has ceased to represent its people's deepest needs. Facing death, the old woman thereby wakens into new awareness and trust, validating the spiritual promise implicit in the title: 'Consider the lilies of the field ...'

That description of an overarching pattern suggests how easily the archetypal approach can mesh with the New Criticism of the 1950s in which the majority of English teachers were trained in the 1960s and later. The characteristic procedure of the teacher as New Critic is to essay a detailed analysis of the complex interrelationships of words, images and symbols within a text read as an organic unity. 'Theme', 'tension', 'pattern of imagery' and 'irony' are typically useful terms for this approach, and of course for Higher Grade English examination responses. It seems to work well for the poetic style of this novel. A valid classroom strategy would be to help students trace the progress of water imagery, for instance, and consider what its repeated evocation in a variety of forms may symbolise in the unconscious life of the protagonist. The inherent danger of such explication of text is boredom for students, who may find such a symbol chase less fascinating than their teacher does, but it can prepare them well for the set text Close Reading questions.

Such mimetic and expressive approaches to a text would be challenged, of course, by any younger teacher trained in the 1970s in a structuralist approach. Feminist readings would be a dimension of this, as would media analysis of conventions, codes and expectations. Vague humanism is to be subverted, and what is tacit or conventional brought into high visibility. The strongly systemic textual conflicts of north–south, Gaelic–Scots, savage–civilised, as well as the discordant codes of dress, physique and manners, and such 'liminal' areas as Glasgow where Highland and Lowland cultures meet and clash (much to the old woman's disgust, when her son brings home a too pert Gaelic girl who has worked as a servant there) are foregrounded. Such tensions can be explored through diagrams or schemata, and I have often found that reluctant students of English, of a mathematical cast of mind, respond quite positively to such codifications of novels. Some of this can usefully be carried out by giving different groups remits to research and report on key areas of conflict.

A central structuring device in *Consider the Lilies* is the choice of a woman's viewpoint by its male author. Structurally in feminist readings, woman is often defined as the negative 'other' to the male voice and vision. This novel, then, gives ample scope to explore issues of dominance and subordination; patriarchal control of religion, family, politics, economics and the law; the construction of masculine characters who are active, dominating, adventurous, rational and creative, as against the female protagonist who seems (at first but not at last) passive, acquiescent, timid, emotional and conventional. There are points of contrast to be made here with other Scottish texts with female voices, real or appropriated, possibly contrasting *Sunset Song* with selected work by A. L. Kennedy, Janice Galloway or Kathleen Jamie. Generally, the 'resisting reader' will counter biases and identify recurrent images of woman in Scottish literature or media, and this may well have an impact on the personal and creative Folio writing done in S5/6 by female candidates.

Reader-response theory is an approach to criticism which many teachers have adopted quite freely because of its links with creative classroom tasks. Focusing on the act of reading as it transpires in the reader's mind, rather than on a meaning inherent and pre-existent in the patterns of the text, the reader is seen as 'co-creative' with the author, particularly where the latter has left gaps or indeterminacies to be filled through prediction, retrospection or reconstruction. The connection with Imaginative Responses to Text at Standard Grade will be clear, and also with imaginative tasks at S1/3 in which pupils adopt the voices of different characters or create subordinate or dependent texts (newspaper articles, wanted posters, diary entries, storyboards and so on) arising from the source text.

A development of reader-response is Stanley Fish's idea of 'interpretative communities' of readers, in which even mistaken readings can contribute to the shared experience of creating an agreed interpretation of the text: there is no single 'right reading'. That sounds uncomfortably close to abrogation of teacherly duty, yet there is also some uneasy evidence that English teachers are not so liberal in approach as they are often reckoned to be, less open to aberrant readings, and inclined in their 'discussion' of texts to focus students specifically towards one sort of acceptable way of discussing texts and coming to conclusions about them (Mitchell, 1992). To that extent, English teachers must always be attempting to balance the examination needs of students (for a certain type of discourse, for a certain sort of insight) against a sense of the richness or plurality of any text.

Or of approaches to it? In the last few decades, Marxist criticism has enjoyed a resurgence, tempered (at least in literary analysis) by an openness to other critical approaches. With its starting point in folk memory of historical change in the means of production, *Consider the Lilies* could be read as an exposure of capitalist ideology, where the owners of the means of production are also seen to control religion, morality and the law. Particularly through the characters of elder and minister, the novel exposes the incoherence and self-delusion lying at the heart of bourgeois morality. This text might even be interpreted as an ironic reconstruction of an earlier subtext, previously silenced and now able to be given voice only in the English/Scots which almost succeeded in erasing it.

Yet the Gaelic voice succeeds in making its mark on the prose rhythms and vocabulary of the text in ways which are interesting to chart and discuss: sometimes there is no word in English to translate what the Gaelic reality means, and we are forced back upon a native lexis which has been well-nigh lost. Again here, the moral implications of the historical tensions between different racial and speech communities in Scotland come close to the surface, and must be addressed by readers.

To that extent, the novel exemplifies in its own unforced way the 'dialogic' quality which the influential Soviet critic, Mikhail Bakhtin, has found in many novels, in which characters are liberated to speak in 'a plurality of independent and unmerged voices', refusing to be smoothed down by the single authoritative authorial voice found in earlier genres. Thus the Gaelic experience is made valid, even for those who cannot speak the language, by Crichton Smith's very choice of the novel form.

In outlining the potential within different critical methods in this way, I am suggesting paths for exploration rather than thorough-going analysis, and also that Scottish literature by its different linguistic nature actually invites an intellectually complex or involved response. Certain teaching methods would therefore follow. Most teachers find that the initial language barrier has to be addressed first. This can be done in several ways. The obvious issues of accent, dialect, audience awareness and context can be set within a developmental framework that reaches back to 5–14 Knowledge about Language strands or, even earlier, to the codes of home and school discourse which can now be reflected upon with some maturity. Memories of Scottish poems and stories read at earlier stages can be revived, particularly if these reveal something of the linguistic diversity of Scottish writing, and of the writer's decision-making about the density and form of Scots to be used. And writers themselves may be heard reading and discussing their work in schools, either through Scottish Arts Council assisted visits, or through taped television programmes or commercial videos.

Another interesting method of teaching the texts is to bring theory and practice together in the sorts of co-creative imaginative responses to text which enact critical theories of reader-response in classroom terms (Protherough, 1983; Corcoran and Evans, 1987; McGonigal, 1992) while also building up Folios of creative work. Cooperative learning techniques of the sort documented in the Standard Grade national development document *Talk about Poetry* (SCCC, 1990) clearly use effective and self-reflective groupwork to develop 'a community of readers' in the post-structuralist manner, while remaining extremely practical.

Finally, the historical, linguistic and social contexts of any Scottish text under discussion can involve students in considering what has endured and what is changing in the Scottish culture which has shaped them. Family relationships, spiritual and moral codes, education and economic life, the memories of older generations passed down in word or music – all of that is a rich source for Folio work in creative or discursive writing, emerging from an understanding which has been shared or shaped in classroom dialogue.

The teaching techniques envisaged for Scottish language and literature, then, are both the same as and yet different from those which teachers would use for English. Crucial issues of personal, community and national identity give an edge to it, and also those myths of severance and recovery in Scottish life which run like fault lines or gold veins below the diverse terrain of our regional writings and national literature.

At the time of writing, the teaching of English post–16 is undergoing its own form of severance. The 'Higher Still' Programme aims to unify current assessment procedures so that Standard Grade, the more vocationally orientated SCOTVEC modules in literature and communication, Higher English and the Certificate of Sixth Year Studies become one system of achievable levels or stages matched to prior attainment. In the process, it is sincerely to be hoped that the advances in Scottish literary and linguistic awareness of the last twenty years will not be lost. A Scottish educational system is surely validated by the very texts it considers worth examining with the next generation, as well as by the adventurous critical or creative approaches our teachers take to them.

BIBLIOGRAPHY

Bold, A., *Modern Scottish Literature* (London: Longman, 1983).

Corcoran, W. and E. Evans, *Readers, Texts, Teachers* (Milton Keynes: Open University Press, 1987).

McGonigal, J., 'Unsettling the Set Text', in E. Evans (ed.), *Young Readers, New Readings* (Hull University Press, 1992).

McGonigal, J., *A Survey of Scottish Texts used in S.5–6 Teaching and Learning* (Glasgow: St Andrew's College, 1997).

Mitchell, S., *Questions and Schooling Classroom Discourse Across the Curriculum*, School of Education Centre for Studies in Rhetoric, Occasional Paper No. 1 (University of Hull, 1992).

Murray, I. and R. Tait, *Ten Modern Scottish Novels* (Aberdeen: Aberdeen University Press, 1984).

Protherough, R., *Developing Responses to Fiction* (Milton Keynes: Open University Press, 1983).

Richards, E., *A History of the Highland Clearances: Agrarian Transformation and the Evictions 1746–1886* (London: Croom Helm, 1982).

SCCC, *Talk About Poetry* (Dundee: Scottish Consultative Council on the Curriculum, 1990).

SEB, *Revised Arrangements in English (Amended) Higher Grade and Certificate of Sixth Year Studies* (Dalkeith: Scottish Examination Board, 1991).

SOED, *Effective Learning and Teaching in Scottish Secondary Schools: English* (Edinburgh: HMSO, 1992).

EXEMPLAR 46

Level/stage of school

S4/6.

Duration

3+ periods.

Topic/text(s)

Reading and talking about poetry: a class video presentation.

Purposes

> To remind pupils that poetry is a communication from poet/speaker to audience.

> To give pupils experience in presenting and talking about poetry to an audience.

Teaching approaches

1. Pupils make a selection of poems for a video programme: general interest, one theme, one poet, etc., as agreed.

2. Allocation of poems to pupil readers; setting up of personal responses, discussions, interviews about the poems by pupils.

3. Rehearsals of readings, interviews, etc.; preparation of reading boards to cue readers on camera; decisions about running order of items; writing of links.

4. Video-recording of poetry programme.

Products

> Video-cassette of class poetry programme (with accompanying texts and notes if desired).

Supporting materials

Recording of sᴛᴠ's *In Verse* (Scottish poetry programme) as possible model (if available).

Critical commentaries on poetry (in print or on audio-cassette) as source of ideas for discussions.

Other comments

This video work can be the culmination of the study of a particular poet or a poetry unit on its own. It should involve a lot of reading, writing and talking.

EXEMPLAR 47

Level/stage of school

S5/6.

Duration

1/2 periods.

Topic/text(s)

As part of a longer study of *Sunset Song* by Lewis Grassic Gibbon, a study of the novel as an interplay of voices.

Purposes

To examine the novel's dialogic nature as part of the writer's narrative technique.

Teaching approaches

1. For ease of working with the topic, a number of different sections can be identified and copied for students to mark and annotate.

2. Suggested sections, with the voices to look for, are:
   (a) Prelude: The Unfurrowed Field (selected paragraphs to show the

voice of the historical storyteller, a general popular voice, a local community voice and individual voices, e.g. Long Rob);

(b) Ploughing: Introduction (six paragraphs, showing a formal voice, a local voice, Chris's voice, other individual voices);

(c) a section of the main narrative showing the folk or community voice, Chris's voice and other individual voices;

(d) Epilude: The Unfurrowed Field (final section from 'Fine weather for January ...', showing the folk voice, individual voices and the minister's formal rhetorical voice).

3. Students should discuss together which voices are being heard in different sections and mark their copies to show the transitions from one voice to another. There should also be discussion of the purposes and contributions of each voice within the contexts of the section and of the novel as a whole.

4. A possible outcome of this study could be the scripting of a section of the novel for a number of readers representing the different voices, and the recording of this as a demonstration of the novel's potential as a play for voices.

5. As part of the larger study of the novel, this topic can be linked to discussions of the place of Chris within the community, Gibbon's use of language, etc.

Products

Students' annotated sections of the novel.

Notes on Gibbon's language, etc.

Other comments

This topic is an application to a well-known novel of the critical thinking of Bakhtin about the modern novel as an interplay of voices.

EXEMPLAR 48

Level/stage at school

S5/6.

Duration

As required.

Topic/text(s)

A cultural study of *Sunset Song* by Lewis Grassic Gibbon.

Purposes

To examine the cultural contents of a major Scottish novel.

Teaching approaches

As part of a more general study of the novel, a number of the following topics can be worked out in detail to set the novel in a number of literary and cultural contexts:

1. *Myth and legend*   The use by Gibbon of a number of mythical themes is very noticeable, the most significant being that of a Golden Age of the past from which humanity has declined. The Diffusionist theory of civilisation has a mythical quality about it that can be related to traditional concepts of Arcadia or Eden, as well as to the philosophy of Rousseau and others. The poetry of Edwin Muir would make a good parallel reference.

   Other traditional themes in *Sunset Song* include the 'Waste Land' motif, in which the land has lost its fertility. Also, the figures of John and Jean Guthrie, and of Ewan and Chris Tavendale, can be seen as representations of the Corn King and Spring Queen figures on whose harmony the fertility depends (as described in *The Golden Bough* by Sir James Frazer).

   The love story of Chris and Ewan is basically a traditional ballad story of the young lovers who are separated by war and the sea, with the man being killed and returning from the dead to be reunited with his love. (See ballads like 'The Wife of Usher's Well', 'Clerk Saunders', etc.)

2. *Scottish history*   Gibbon uses Scottish history as a constant background to his story in *Sunset Song*. There are: the historical background of Kinraddie as outlined in the Prelude; the visions of historical figures, the Pict hailing the sight of the ships of Pytheas and the warrior of Calgacus's army; Chris's perceptions of the cruelties endured by the common people of Scotland at the hands of their overlords; the evocation of William Wallace as a popular hero; and the pervading idealisation of the Picts as the traditional Scots folk. Gibbon's vision of Scottish history is a bleak

one; he does not subscribe to the flattering romantic myths of Scotland's past, but fits it into his thesis of the decline of human happiness from a lost Golden Age. Gibbon argues all this out fully in essays in the important survey of Scotland he produced with Hugh MacDiarmid, *Scottish Scene.*

3. *The rural way of life* The most memorable images of *Sunset Song* are of the work on the land in the different seasons. As an evocation of the traditional farming in rural Lowland Scotland, it has probably never been bettered. There is a lot of similar writing about rural Scotland that can be referred to, but the significant thing about Gibbon's writing is his sense of this way of life as being a degrading toil that imprisons the spirits of those who depend on it. Gibbon's essay 'The Land' in *Scottish Scene* is a crucial document here. Gibbon's links with other rural novelists are worth exploring, e.g. Thomas Hardy. An entertaining parody of the fashionable rural novel genre, *Cold Comfort Farm* by Stella Gibbons (interesting similarity), is worth referring to also.

4. *Popular literature* Immediate links can be made between *Sunset Song* and popular entertainment in Scotland. The most obvious is with traditional Scots songs (and other popular traditional songs) through the figure of Long Rob and his role in the novel as a cultural symbol, carrying on the song tradition, which is lost on his death in the war. Chris is important also through her association with 'The Flowers of the Forest', a symbol of Scotland's past and the loss and defeat that are part of that past. A dimension of study can be opened up based on this song tradition. Equally there is the tradition of the Bothy Ballads, which were songs and stories coming out of the farming communities of the north-east. A lot of the background of anecdote and reminiscence in the novel has associations with this popular tradition. Hearing some of this material would be a valuable adjunct to the study of the novel.

5. *Calvinism and sexuality* The way in which religion is presented in the novel, and the warping of John Guthrie's character by extreme Calvinism, is an important dimension of the novel. Immediate links can be made with poems like 'Holy Willie's Prayer' and 'The Holy Fair' by Burns, and 'The Scarecrow' by Derick Thomson. It would be worthwhile to consider all the different representations of ministers in the novel, from the old minister Mr Greig referred to at the beginning down to Robert Colquhoun at the end, to see how Gibbon has charted the declining influence of the Kirk in the period covered by the novel.

6. *The Great War (1914–18)* The presentation of the war in the novel is an indirect one, showing its effects on the home community rather than the horrors of the trenches. However, the psychological effects on Ewan and the deaths of Chae and Long Rob link with the familiar themes of war poetry and autobiography. As well as reading the usual Owen, Brooke and Sassoon, there is a Scottish body of First World War poetry that

should be familiar to teachers and students. An anthology like *In Flanders Fields* edited by Trevor Royle is an indispensable collection for studying this topic in class. The poems of Ewart Alan Mackintosh, Joseph Lee and Charles Hamilton Sorley should be as much read in Scottish schools as the English poets. Supplemented by stories of the Scottish regiments in the war, photographs of the time and the poetry referred to, *Sunset Song* can be part of a study of the theme, 'The Horror of War').

7. *Political idealism*   Gibbon's political ideals are explicit throughout the novel. Without being distracted too much by the Marxist bias of his thesis, teachers can examine how the novel expresses anger at the unjust system that fetters the spirits and lives of the people of Kinraddie, and how characters like John Guthrie, Chae Strachan, Long Rob, Robert Colquohoun, Maggie Jean Gordon, etc., express opposition to the political and economic situation. Marxism is not really an issue in *Sunset Song*; that is for the later novels of *A Scots Quair*. The idealistic Socialism of Chae and Robert is the hoped-for alternative, linking with the Golden Age that is lost. However, some of the poetry of MacDiarmid and other poets of the Scottish Renaissance can be read in parallel with the novel.

8. *Literary modernism*   An often neglected aspect of *Sunset Song* is its status as a novel of the 1930s, a text in the new Modernist wave. It is not a traditional novel, although it contains traditional aspects and themes. In its language (which Gibbon himself saw as paralleling the experiments of Hugh MacDiarmid and James Joyce), in its anti-kailyard and anti-traditional aspects, in its use of myth and archetypes (influenced by Frazer and Jung, and akin to what Eliot had done in 'The Waste Land'), and in its political and social commitment, it is a novel of its time. A reading of poems and stories of the 1930s will show up many interesting parallels. The poetry of MacDiarmid and Soutar, and the early prose of Naomi Mitchison, Neil Gunn and Eric Linklater, will produce fruitful connections.

EXEMPLAR 49

Level/stage of school

S4/5.

Duration

3 to 4 periods.

Topic/text(s)

Study of three poems: 'Poem for My Sister', by Liz Lochhead; 'Fellow Passenger', by Valerie Gillies; 'Plainsong', by Carol Ann Duffy.

Purposes

To improve skills in responding to rhythm and image in poetry.

To introduce students to a range of women's writing.

To demonstrate that women's writing is diverse and not restricted to so-called 'women's issues'.

Teaching approaches

1. Read all three poems with the class, preferably in the order given above. These are all poems by women writers but display diverse areas of interest. Establish with the class what these areas are. What contrasts and comparisons emerge?

2. The first line of 'Poem for My Sister' can be read to sound like a playground skipping rhyme and is appropriate for a poem which wishes to express the innocence and funniness of childhood. Students could write a poem about a childhood experience using Lochhead's rhythm for their first line.

3. Show the class how the metaphor of shoes and feet develops 'Poem for My Sister's' theme and use this as the introduction to 'Fellow Passenger' which builds up a picture of a man's job and character in a series of images. Ask the class to write an entry on Mr Rajan for his firm's personnel file using the information gleaned from the poem's images. Or ask students to write a letter from one of Mr Rajan s daughters to a cousin in which she describes her father.

4. 'Plainsong' is a difficult poem to understand because it uses a personal symbolism which the poem does not explain. It can be read as an autobiographical reaction to the poet's adoption. Help the class to work out as much as they can. The poem does have a very strong sense of emotion linked to place. Rather than spending too much time on *why* the poet feels as she does, encourage students to compile a list of *what* she feels and how that is expressed through landscape. Although pupils may feel dissatisfied because they have not fully 'understood' the poem, reassure them that with some poetry a partial interpretation and a sense of something indefinable is an appropriate response.

Products

Creative writing essays.

A set of notes on the first two poems which may be used as the basis of examination answers.

An RPR discussing similarities and dissimilarities among all three poems.

Supporting materials

Copies of the poems.

Other comments

The references in 'Fellow Passenger' to Venkateswaran and Sai Babi are taken from Hinduism. The temple of Venkatesa is situated at Tirupati in southern India. There is some dispute over whether it is dedicated to Vishnu or Siva but it is generally regarded as being one of the three most important Vishnu temples in South India. The Sai Babi movement reveres Sai Babi as the reincarnation of a nineteenth-century mystic, Sirdi Sai Babi, and an incarnation of Siva. The chief effect of these references is to emphasise Mr Rajan's active Hindu observance.

EXEMPLAR 50

Level/stages of school

S5/6.

Duration

As required.

Topic/text(s)

Study of the novel *The Trick Is To Keep Breathing,* by Janice Galloway for students' RPR or for CSYS dissertation, perhaps in addition to another related novel.

Purposes

To encourage students to get to grips with fractured narrative technique.

To enable students to think critically about emotive issues such as grief, images of women in society generally and how they relate specifically to eating disorders.

Teaching approaches

A novel which deals with anorexia and bulimia, depression and a series of sexual relationships expressing these issues in strong language may not be the book everyone wants to read. These issues, however, are regularly discussed in teen magazines and women's magazines. It is unlikely this novel will tell students anything that they do not already know. However, the novel can illuminate these issues imaginatively and critically.

1. Ask students to read the text in their own time and note their own first responses to it. The narrative structure is more like that of a film than a conventional novel with flashbacks, repeated significant images and glimpses of the future. Ask them to unravel the narrative and retell it in chronological order. In order to help them understand how the novel's narrative expresses Joy's disturbed consciousness so well, ask them to think about why Galloway chooses to not to tell Joy's story chronologically.

2. The novel is not conventionally printed. Sometimes there are notes in the margin, sometimes there are lists, sections in italics, or a series of 'ooo's which act as section markers. For some students it may be appropriate to introduce them to the term 'postmodernism' which accounts for such changes. For other students it may be appropriate to let them work out the meanings by analogy with youth television which often uses a fast-moving variety of styles to communicate.

3. Discuss the emotions Joy feels in order to work out why these universal emotions lead her into such a dark situation. Such discussion could provide stimulus for personal writing.

4. Provide a selection of women's/teen magazines. In the novel women's magazines are used ironically to show the contrast between women's lives as they might be and as they are. Discuss the major contradiction between 'recipes' – where women are providers and consumers of food – and 'diets' – where women are expected to abstain voluntarily from food. Look at horoscopes, agony columns and readers' 'personal experiences' and highlight the contrast between fantasy and reality. (This exercise might be done with the whole class or with a group working on images of women for discursive essays.)

Products

> A set of notes on the novel.
>
> A set of notes for discursive writing.
>
> Personal writing.
>
> An RPR essay.

Supporting materials

> A selection of magazines.

Other comments

While it is likely that girls may be more drawn to these issues than boys, it is important that boys should not feel excluded. It is not axiomatic that the terms of existence of one gender are of no interest to the other. Boys may find female perspectives illuminating and may wish to explore issues of male identity in similar ways – a less obvious but entirely necessary area of study.

Appendices

APPENDIX A
WRITING WORKSHOPS

The development of pupils' imaginative writing is one of the primary concerns of teachers at all stages of the school. The setting up of writing workshops, which operate on a regular basis over a set period of time, is one of the best ways to create a supportive cooperative environment within which pupils can discuss ideas for writing and begin the writing process, read and discuss their own work, and hear and discuss the work of their companions in the group. In this workshop, the teacher generally functions as a member of the group, writing and discussing along with the others (depending on the age and maturity of the group as a whole), and is not acting as an ultimate authority. Helpful comment and criticism should come from the group as a whole.

To provide suggestions about possible topics and approaches using Scottish materials, there follows three exemplars, one for each main stage of the secondary school.

EXEMPLAR 51

Level/stage of school

S5/6.

Duration

As desired.

Topic/text(s)

New Writing Scotland (Association for Scottish Literary Studies, annually).

Purposes

To make students aware of contemporary writing activity in Scotland.

To encourage students to write with possible publishing outlet in mind.

Teaching approaches

1. Make copies of NWS (different issues or multiple copies of one issue - back numbers may be obtainable from ASLS at reduced price) available to students for general reading over a few days. Ask them to pick one or two pieces that particularly appeal to them.

2. Hold a reading session at which teacher and students read their favourite pieces and discuss them.

3. Discuss the kinds and styles of writing that students feel to be most effective and/or entertaining.

4. Set up a short series of writing workshops to which students bring short pieces they have written to be read out and discussed helpfully. (The teacher should take part as both a writer and a reader.)

5. Set up small editorial board of students to select a number of pieces that might be submitted for publication in NWS (submissions before end of January). Send off pieces in accordance with NWS requirements.

Products

Students' edited writing.

Other comments

Students should also be introduced at some point in their course to other Scottish literary magazines, e g *Chapman, Cencrastus, West Coast Magazine,* etc

EXEMPLAR 52

Level/stage of school

S2 or S3.

Duration

5+ periods.

Topic/text(s)

A major writing project: class 'episodic novel' based on ballad sources.

Purposes

> To engage the pupils in a major group writing project that will produce a continuing story involving a small group of invented characters who have adventures inspired by ballad stories.
>
> To involve the pupils in the reading of a number of traditional ballads as an imaginative stimulus for talk and writing.

Teaching Approaches

1. Select a number of ballads (e.g. from *Scottish Ballads*) as sources of stories to write about.

2. Introduce the topic to pupils as a kind of continuing 'romance' or 'serial adventure'. Create a small group of characters as the centre of the fiction (e.g. a wandering knight, Sir Andrew; a young gentlewoman, Lady Maisry, who has become separated from her family; a poor friar begging his way from village to village). Engage the pupils in the idea that they are going to write their adventures as they encounter the situations of different ballads.

3. Distribute ballads to groups of pupils (one ballad to each group of three or four) for the pupils to read and discuss stories. Pupils discuss how one or more of the created characters will become involved in the ballad story.

4. Pupils work out the basic outline of their episodes and begin writing, part cooperatively and part individually, using a variety of formats – eye-witness accounts, journal entries, interviews, letters, third-person narratives, etc. Collect the stories together in a chronological sequence as they are completed. Finish when project runs out of steam.

Products

An episodic, diverse fiction embodying work by all the pupils. Can be illustrated as desired, with maps, pictures, illuminated capitals (as in manuscripts), etc.

Supporting materials

Prints and pictures of Arthurian romance situations (e.g. by Pre-Raphaelite artists).

Other comments

This may seem overly-ambitious, but the teacher can keep it under control to make the product as long as is practicable. Think in terms of Spenser, Malory, Ariosto.

EXEMPLAR 53

Level/stage at school

S3/4.

Duration

As desired.

Topic/text(s)

Writing project – stimulus: 'Windows in the West', watercolour picture by Avril Paton.

Purposes

To encourage varied writing from an artistic stimulus.

Teaching approaches

1. Display poster or circulate cards, and elicit opinions on the picture – season of year, setting, social level of area, time of day, etc.

2. Move on to identify the individual flats and discuss what may be happening in the different rooms, especially those that are lit up. Pupils make notes about possibilities.

3. Each group takes a floor of the tenement building, and each pupil in the group takes a different room. Pupils write their own accounts of what is happening in their chosen room – third-person narrative, first-person narrative, dramatic sketch, verse, etc.

4. Hold reading sessions to give the class a sense of the life of the whole building. Discuss the different pieces |and the overall picture of the occupancy of the flats.

5. Pupils polish up their writing and put into final draft for collection into an anthology, 'The Tenement' or some other suitable title.

6. Extend the writing into other forms and into other speculations about the life of the building.

Products

Pupils's individual writings.

A class anthology or 'novel'.

Other comments

Parallel reading – novels and stories such as *The Tenement* (Iain Crichton Smith), *That Rubens Guy* (John McGill), etc.

APPENDIX B
SOURCES OF TEXTS IN EXEMPLARS

SOURCES OF TOPIC/TEXT(S)

1. 'Tam o' Shanter' (Robert Burns): in any good Burns edition.
2. *Sunset Song* (Lewis Grassic Gibbon): Canongate Classics and other editions.
3. 'Feathered Choristers' (Brian McCabe): in *The Devil and the Giro*, ed. Carl MacDougall, Canongate Classics.
4. 'Epitaph for an Army of Mercenaries' (A. E. Housman): in *Oxford Book of English Verse*.
   'Another Epitaph on an Army of Mercenaries' (Hugh MacDiarmid): in any good MacDiarmid edition.
   'A Third Epitaph on an Army of Mercenaries' (Edwin Morgan): in *Sweeping Out the Dark* (Carcanet, 1994) or *Collected Poems*.
5. 'The Wife of Usher's Well' (Anon.): in *Scottish Ballads*, ed. Emily Lyle, Canongate Classics, and many other anthologies.
6. Extract on 'Macbeth': from *The Chronicles of Scotland*, compiled by Hector Boece and translated into Scots by John Bellenden (1531), STS III.15, p. 149 – see Appendix C.
7. *Ane Pleasaunt Satyre of the Thrie Estaitis* (Sir David Lyndsay): ed. Roderick Lyall, Canongate Classics.
8. Poems in 'Standard Habbie' form: in the *Penguin Book of Scottish Verse*, ed. Tom Scott, and other anthologies.
9. 'The Twa Dogs' (Robert Burns): in any good Burns edition.
10. *Concise Scots Dictionary* (Chambers); any Gaelic dictionary.
11. *Scots Saws* (David Murison): Mercat Press, 1981; *A Collection of Scots Proverbs* (Allan Ramsay, 1750): reprinted by Paul Harris Publishing, 1979.
12. Extract, 'Summons of the Doomed of Flodden (Robert Lindsay of Pitscottie): *History*, XX.xvii (*a.* 1575) – see Appendix C.
13. Extract, 'St Giles' Day Riot in Edinburgh' (John Knox): from *History of the Reformation in Scotland* (in David Laing (ed.), *The Works of John Knox*, Edinburgh, 1846, I.258 ff.) – see Appendix C.
15. 'The Lost Pibroch' (Neil Munro): in *The Lost Pibroch, and Other Shieling Stories*, 1896, reprinted by House of Lochar, 1996.

Para Handy (Neil Munro): in *Para Handy and other tales* by Hugh Foulis (Neil Munro), Hutchinson, and other editions.

16. 'Coffins' (Derick Thomson): in *Modern Scottish Gaelic Poems* (Nua-Bhardachd Ghaidhlig), ed. Donald MacAulay, Canongate.

17. The Wedding' (Iain Crichton Smith): in *The Black and the Red*, Gollancz, and *A Third Book of Modern Scottish Stories*, eds R. Millar and J. T. Low, Heinemann Educational Books (out of print).

18. 'How the First Hielandman was Made' (Anon.): in *The Ring of Words*, eds A. MacGillivray and J. Rankin, Oliver & Boyd – see Appendix C.

19. *The Kist/A' Chiste*: SCCC/Nelson Blackie, 1996.

20. *Concise Scots Dictionary*, Chambers.

21. *The Scots Thesaurus*, Chambers.

22. 'This is thi six a clock news' (Tom Leonard): in *Twelve More Modern Scottish Poets*, ed. C. King, Hodder & Stoughton.

23. 'Sisyphus' (Robert Garioch): in *Twelve Modern Scottish Poets*, ed. C. King, Hodder & Stoughton.
    Extract, 'The Glasgow Swordsman in Hades', from *The Bridge* (Iain Banks), Futura Books (now Orbit Books), pp. 159–68.

24. 'The Taill of the Uponlandis Mous and the Burges Mous' (Robert Henryson): in the *Oxford Book of Scottish Verse* and other Scottish anthologies.

25. 'A Counterblaste against Tobacco' (James VI): *Medieval Scots Prose*, ed. R. D. S. Jack, Calder & Boyars – see Appendix C.

26. 'Stobhill' (Edwin Morgan): in *Selected Poems* and *Collected Poems*, Carcanet.

27. *Free Love* (Ali Smith): Virago Original.

28. 'Where the Debris Meets the Sea' (Irvine Welsh): in *The Acid House*, Jonathan Cape.

29. *Laidlaw* (William McIlvanney): Coronet/Hodder & Stoughton.

30. Novels of Iain Banks and Iain M. Banks under various paperback imprints, e.g. Futura, Abacus and Orbit.

31. 'The Taill of the Uponlandis Mous and the Burges Mous' (Robert Henryson): in *Selected Poems of Henryson and Dunbar*, eds P. Bawcutt and F. Riddy, Scottish Academic Press, and as for Exemplar 24.

32. Scottish Renaissance sonnets in various collections, especially *The Scottish Collection of Verse to 1800* eds E. Dunlop and A. Kamm, Richard Drew – see Appendix C.
    Sonnets by Robert Garioch: in *Collected Poems* and various anthologies, e.g. *Twelve Modern Scottish Poets*, ed. C. King, Hodder & Stoughton.
    'Glasgow Sonnets' (Edwin Morgan): in *Selected Poems* and *Collected Poems*, Carcanet.

33. *Sonnets from Scotland* (Edwin Morgan): Mariscat Press; also in *Themes on a Variation* and *Collected Poems*, Carcanet.

34. Satirical poems of Robert Burns: in any good Burns edition.

35. 'Tam o' Shanter' (Robert Burns): in any good Burns edition.

36. 'Letter to Mrs Dunlop, 22 March, 1787' (Collected Letters of Burns, CL

134-5): in *Rhymer Rab: an anthology of poems and prose by Robert Burns*, ed. Alan Bold, London: Black Swan Books, 1993.

'Epistle to William Simson' (Robert Burns): in any good Burns edition.

37. *The Kist/A'Chiste*, SCCC/Nelson Blackie, anthology and pack of teaching materials.

38. *Scots School Dictionary*, *Pocket Scots Dictionary* and *Concise Scots Dictionary*: Chambers.

39. *Scots School Dictionary*: Chambers; *The New English Gaelic Dictionary* (Derick Thomson): Gairm Publications.

40. 'Tam o' Shanter' (Robert Burns): in any good Burns edition.

41. 'Lament for the Makaris' (William Dunbar): in the *Penguin Book of Scottish Verse*, ed. Tom Scott, and other anthologies.

42. 'Lamkin' (Anon.): in *Scottish Ballads*, ed. Emily Lyle, Canongate Classics.

43. 'Elegy on Maggy Johnston' (Allan Ramsay): in *Selected Poems of Ramsay and Fergusson*, eds A. M. Kinghorn and A. Law, Scottish Academic Press.

44. 'Peggy's Walk' (Pat Gerber): in *Maiden Voyage*, Glasgow: Kailyards Press.

45. 'The Bottle Imp' (Robert Louis Stevenson): in *Selected Short Stories of R. L. Stevenson*, ed. I. Campbell, Ramsay Head Press, and other collections of Stevenson's stories.

47. *Sunset Song* (Lewis Grassic Gibbon): Canongate Classics.

48. As for Exemplar 47.

49. 'Poem for my Sister' (Liz Lochhead): in *Dreaming Frankenstein and Collected Poems*, Polygon.

'Fellow Passenger' (Valerie Gillies) and 'Plainsong' (Carol Ann Duffy): in *The Faber Book of Twentieth Century Scottish Poetry*.

50. *The Trick is to Keep Breathing* (Janice Galloway): Edinburgh: Polygon, 1989.

51. *New Writing Scotland*, published annually by Association for Scottish Literary Studies (14 issues produced up to 1996).

53. Painting, 'Windows in the West': watercolour by Avril Paton, in Glasgow Gallery of Modern Art; posters and cards available from Glasgow art galleries and museums.

SOURCES OF FURTHER SUPPORTING MATERIAL

5. D. E. Adland, *The Group Approach to Drama*, 6 vols, London: Longmans, various dates.

14. D. Dorward, *Scotland's Place Names*, Edinburgh: Mercat Press, 1996.

W. F. H. Nicolaisen, *Scottish Placenames*, London: Batsford, 1976.

17. R. Millar and J. T. Low, *A Third Book of Modern Scottish Stories*, Heinemann Educational Books (out of print).

34. J. Hodgart, *Robert Burns: Study Guide for Revised Higher*, ASLS, 1993.

35. Hodgart (1993) – as for Exemplar 34.

K. Simpson, *Robert Burns*, Scotnotes No. 9, ASLS.
48. L. G. Gibbon and H. MacDiarmid, *Scottish Scene*, London: Hutchinson, 1934.
    S. Gibbons, *Cold Comfort Farm*, London: Longman, 1932.
    T. Royle, *In Flanders Fields*, Edinburgh: Mainstream.
52. E. Lyle (ed.), *Scottish Ballads*, Canongate Classics.
53. Iain Crichton Smith, *The Tenement*.
    John McGill, *That Rubens Guy*, Edinburgh: Mainstream, 1990.

SOURCES OF SUPPORT REFERENCE WORKS

Abair!: Faclair (Dictionary), eds R. W. Renton and J. A. MacDonald, Glasgow: Mingulay Publications, 1979.

The Concise English–Scots Dictionary, eds I. Macleod and P. Cairns, Edinburgh: Chambers, 1993.

The Concise Scots Dictionary, ed. M. Robinson, Aberdeen: Aberdeen University Press, 1985.

Illustrated Gaelic–English Dictionary, ed. E. Dwelly, London, 1911.

The New English–Gaelic Dictionary, ed. D. S. Thomson, Glasgow: Gairm Publications, 1986.

The Pocket Scots Dictionary, eds I. Macleod, R. Martin and P. Cairns, Aberdeen: Aberdeen University Press, 1988.

A Pronouncing and Etymological Dictionary of the Gaelic Language, ed. M. MacLennan, Aberdeen: Acair and Aberdeen University Press, 1979.

The Scots School Dictionary, eds I. Macleod and P. Cairns, Edinburgh: Chambers, 1996.

The Scots Thesaurus, eds I. Macleod, P. Cairns, C. Macafee and R. Martin, Aberdeen: Aberdeen University Press, 1990 (now published by Chambers).

APPENDIX C
EXTRACTS

'MACBETH'

Off the weirdis gevin to Makbeth and Banquho; how Makbeth was maid Thayne of Cauder, and how he slew King Duncan to mak him self king.

The same tyme happynnit ane wounderfull thing. Quhen Makbeth and Banquho war passand to Fores, quhair King Duncan wes for the tyme, thai mett be the gaits thre weird sisteris or wiches, quhilk come to thame with elrege clething. The first of thame sayid to Makbeth: "Haill, Thayne of Glammys!" The secund sayid: "Hayill, Thayn of Cawder" The thrid sayid: "Haill, Makbeth, that salbe sum tyme King of Scotlannd!" Than said Banquho: "Quhat wemen be ʒe, quhilkis bene sa vnmercifull to me and sa propiciant to my companeoun, gevand him nocht onlie landis and grete rentis bot als triumphand kingdome, and gevis me nocht?" To this ansuerit the first of thir wiches: "Wee schaw mair feliciteis appering to the than to him; for thocht he happin to be ane king, ʒite his empyre sall end vnhappely, and nane of his blude sall eftir him succede. Be contrair, thou sall neuer be king, bot of the sall cum mony kingis, quhilkis with lang and ancient lynage sall reioise the crovun of Scotland.". Thir wourdis beand sayid, thai suddanlye evanyst oute of their sycht.

This prophecy & diuinacioun was haldin lang in derisioun to Banquho and Makbeth, for sum tyme Banquho wald call Makbeth "King of Scottis" for derisioun, and he on the samyn maner wald call Banquho "The fader of mony kingis.". Nochttheles, becaus all thingis come as thir wiches divinit, the pepill traistit thame to be werd sisteris. Schort tyme eftir, the Thayne of Cawder wes disheresit of his landis for certane crymes of leis maieste, and his lanais wer geven be King Duncan to Makbeth. It happynnit the nixt nycht that Banquho and Makbeth war sportand to giddir at their suppair. Than said Banquho: "Thou has gottin all that the first twa sisteris hecht; restis nocht bot the croun, quhilk was hecht be the thrid sister." Makbeth, revolwyug all thingis as thai war said be thir wyches, began to covaitt the crovun, nochtheles, thocht best to abyde quhill he saw his tyme, and tuke sikkir esperance that the thrid werde suld cum to him, as the first twa did afoir.

In the menetyme King Duncan maid his son Macolme Prince of Cumbir, to signifye that he suld regnne eftir him; quhilk thing wes importabill

206

displeser to Makbeth, for it maid plane derogacioun to the thrid weir promittit afoir to him be thir werede sisteris.

From *The Chronicles of Scotland*, compiled by Hector Boece and translated into Scots by John Bellenden.

'SUMMONS OF THE DOOMED OF FLODDEN'

Thair was a cry hard at the marcat crose of Edinburgh at the houre of midnight proclamand as it had bene ane sowmondis quhilk was nameit and callit be the proclamer thairof the sowmondis of Plotcok, quhilk desyrit all men to compeir baith earle, lord, barone and gentillmen and all honest burgessis within the toune, ewerie man specifeit be his awin name to compeir within the space of fourtie day befoir his maister quhair it sall happin him to appoynt and be for the tyme under the paine of dissobedience. Bot quhither thir sowmondis war proclaimeit be waine personis night walkeris or dronkin men for thar pastyme, or gif it was bot a spreit as I have schawin to 3ow befoir, I can not tell trewlie: bot it was schawin to me that ane nobill man of the toun callit Maister Richart Lawson beand evil dispossit gangand in his gallerie stair foment the corse, heirand this woce proclamand this sowmondis thocht marwell quhat it sould be, cryit on his serwant to bring him his purse, and quhen he brought him it he tuik out ane croune and cast it ower the stair sayand thir wordis as efter followis:- "I appeill frae that sowmondis judgement and sentance theirof and takis me all haill in the marcie of God and Christ Jesis his sone."... Thair was no maner of man that eskaipit that was callit in that summoundis bot that ane man alane quhilk maid his protestatioun and appeillit frae the saidis sowmoundis bot all the laif was perischit in the feild [Flodden] with the kings grace.

Extract from Robert Lindsay of Pitscottie, *History*.

'ST GILES' DAY RIOT IN EDINBURGH'

But yit could the Bischoppes in no sorte be qwyet; for Sanct Geillis day approcheing, their gave charge to the Provest, Baillies, and Counsall of Edinburgh, eyther to gett agane the ald Sanct Geile, or ellis upoun thaire expenssis to maik ane new image. The Counsall answered, "That to thame the charge appeired verray injust; for thei understood that God in some plaices had commanded idolles and images to be distroyed; but where he had commanded ymages to be sett up, thei had nott read; and desyred the Bischope to fynd a warrant for his commandiment." Whareat the Bischope offended, admonissed under pane of curssing; which thei prevented by a formall Appellatioun; appelling from him, as from a parciall and corrupt judge, unto the Pape's holynes; and so grettar thingis schortly following, that passed in oblivioun. Yit wold nott the Preastis and Freiris cease to have that great solempnitie and manifest abhominatioun which thei accustomablie had upoun Sanct Geillis day, to witt, their wold have that idole borne; and tharefor was all preparatioun necessar deuly maid. A marmouset idole was borrowed fra the Gray Freiris, (a silver peise of James Carmichaell was laid in pledge:) It was fast fixed with irne nailles upon a barrow, called thare fertour. Thare assembled Preastis, Frearis, Channonis, and rottin Papistes, with tabornes and trumpettis, banerris and bage-pypes, and who was thare to led the ring, but the Quein Regent hir self, with all hir schaivelingis, for honour of that feast. West about goes it, and cumis doun the Hie Streat, and doun to the Canno Croce. The Quein Regent dyned that day in Sandie Carpetyne's housse, betuix the Bowes, and so when the idole returned back agane, scho left it, and past in to hir dennar. The heartes of the brethrein war wonderouslie inflammed, and seing such abominatioun so manifestlie manteaned, war decreed to be revenged. Thei war devided in severall cumpanyes, wharof not one knew of ane other. Thare war some temperisaris that day, (amonges whome David Forress, called the Generall, was one,) who, fearing the chance to be dune as it fell, laubored to stay the brethrein. Butt that could not be; for immediatlie after that the Quein was entered in the loodgeing, some of those that war of the interprise drew ney to the idole, as willing to helpe to bear him, and getting the fertour upon thare schulderis, begane to schudder, thinking that thairby the idole should have fallin. But that was provided and prevented by the irne nailles, as we have said; and so, begane one to cry "Doun with the idole; doun with it;" and so without delay it was pulled doun. Some brag maid the Preastis patrons at the first; but when thei saw the febilness of thare god, (for one took him by the heillis, and cladding his head to the calsay, left Dagon without head or handis, and said, "Fye upon thee, thow young Sanct Geile, thy father wold half taryed four such:") this considered, (we say,) the Preastis and Freiris fled faster then thei did at Pynckey Clewcht [Battle of Pinkie]. Thare mycht have bein sein so suddane a fray as seildome hes bein sein amonges that sorte of men within this realme; for doun goes the croses, of goes the surpleise, round cappes corner with the crounes. The Gray Freiris gapped, the Blak Frearis blew, the Preastis panted, and fled, and happy was he that first gate the house; for such ane sudden fray came never amonges the generatioun of Antichrist within this realme befoir. By chance thare lay upoun a stare a meary Englissman, and seing the discomfiture to be without blood, thought he wold add some mearynes to the mater, and so cryed he ower a stayr, and said, "Fy upoun yow, hoorsones, why have ye brockin ordour! Doun the street ye passed in array and with great myrth. Why flie ye, vilanes, now, without ordour? Turne and stryk everie one a strok for the honour of his god. Fy, cowardis, fy, ye shall never be judged worthy of your wages agane!" But exhortationis war then unprofitable; for after that Bell [Baal] had brokin his neck, thare was no conforte to his confused army.

Extract from John Knox, *The History of the Reformation in Scotland.*

'HOW THE FIRST HIELANDMAN WAS MADE'

God and Saint Peter was gangand be the way
Heich up in Argyll where their gait lay.
Saint Peter said to God, in ane sport word -
'Can ye nocht mak a Hielandman of this horse turd?'
God turned owre the horse turd with his pykit staff,   5
And up start a Hielandman black as ony draff.
Quod God to the Hielandman, 'Where wilt thou now?'
'I will doun in the Lawland, Lord, and there steal a cow.'
'And thou steal a cow, carle, there they will hang thee.'
'What reck, Lord, of that, for anis mon I die.'   10
God then he leuch and owre the dyke lap,
And out of his sheath his gully outgat.
Saint Peter socht the gully fast up and doun,
Yet could not find it in all that braid roun.
'Now,' quod God, 'here a marvel, how can this be,   15
That I suld want my gully, and we here bot three.'
'Humf,' quod the Hielandman, and turned him about,
And at this plaid neuk the gully fell out.
'Fy,' quod Saint Peter, 'thou will never do weill;
And thou bot new made and sa soon gais to steal.'   20
'Humf,' quod the Hielandman, and sware be yon kirk,
'Sa lang as I may gear get to steal, I will never wirk.'

                                               (Anon.)

'A COUNTERBLAST AGAINST TOBACCO'

And now good cuntrey-men, let us (I pray you) consider, what honour or policy can moove us to imitate the barbarous and beastly maners of the wilde, godlesse, and slavish Indians, especially in so vile and stinking a custome? Shall we that disdaine to imitate the maners of our neighbour France (having the stile of the first Christian kingdome) and that cannot endure the spirit of the Spaniards (their King being now comparable in largenesse of dominions, to the great Emperour of Turkie); shall wee, I say, that have bene so long civill and wealthy in peace, famous and invincible in warre, fortunate in both, we that have bene ever able to aide any of our neighbours (but never deafed any of their eares with any of our supplications for assistance) shall wee, I say, without blushing, abase our selves so farre, as to imitate these beastly Indians, slaves to the Spaniards, refuse to the world, and as yet aliens from the holy covenant of God? Why doe we not as well imitate them in walking naked as they doe, in preferring glasses, feathers, and such toyes, to gold and precious stones, as they doe, yea why doe we not denie God and adore the divel, as they doe?

The other argument drawn from a mistaken experience, is but the more particular probation of this generall, because it is alledged to be found trew by proofe, that by the taking of tobacco divers and very many doe finde themselves cured of divers diseases as on the other part, no man ever received harme thereby. In this argument there is first a great mistaking and next a monstrous absurditie, for is it not a very great mistaking, to take *non causam pro causa*, as they say in the Logickes? Because peradventure, when a sicke man hath had his disease at the height, hee hath at that instant taken tobacco, and afterward his disease taking the naturall course of declining, and consequently the patient of recovering his health, O then the tobacco forsooth, was the worker of that miracle. Beside that, it is a thing well known to all physicians, that the apprehension and conceit of the patient, hath by wakening and uniting the vitall spirits, and so strengthening nature, a great power and vertue, to cure divers diseases. For an evident proofe of mistaking in the like case, I pray you what foolish boy, what sillie wench, what olde doting wife, or ignorant countrey clowne, is not a physician for the toothach, for the cholicke and divers such common diseases? Yea, will not every man you meete withall, teach you a sundry cure for the same, and sweare by that meane either himselfe, or some of his neerest kinsemen and friends was cured? And yet I hope no man is so foolish as to beleeve them. And all these toyes do only proceed from the mistaking *non causam pro causa*, as I have already said, and so if a man chance to recover one of any disease, after hee hath taken tobacco, that must have the thanks of all. But by the contrary, if a man smoke himselfe to death with it (and many have done) O then some other disease must beare the blame for that fault. So doe olde harlots thanke their harlotrie for their many yeeres, that custome being healthfull (say they) *ad purgandos renes*, but never have mind how many die of the pockes in the flower of their youth. And so doe olde drunkards thinke they prolong their dayes, by their swinelike diet, but never remember how many die drowned in drinke before they be halfe olde.

And what greater absurditie can there be, then to say that one cure shall serve for divers, nay, contrarious sorts of diseases? It is an undoubted ground among all physicians, that there is almost no sort either of nourishment or medicine, that hath not some thing in it disagreeable to some part of mans bodie, because, as I have alreadie said, the nature of the temperature of every part, is so different from another, tbat according to the olde proverbe, that which is good for the head is evill for the necke and the shoulders. For even as a strong enemy, that invades a town or fortresse, although in his siege thereof, he do belay and compasse it round about, yet he makes his breach and entry at some one or fewe speciall parts thereof, which hee hath tried and found to be weakest and least able to resist; so sickenes doth make her particular assault, upon such part or parts of our body, as are weakest and easiest to be overcome by that sort of disease, which then doth assaile us, although all the rest of tbe body by sympathie feele it selfe, to be as it were belayed, and besieged by the affliction of that speciall part, the griefe and smart thereof being by the sense of feeling dispersed through all the rest of our members. And therefore the skilfull physician presses by such cures, to purge and strengthen that part which is afflicted, as are only fit for that sort of disease, and doe best agree with the nature of that infirme part; which being abused to a disease of another nature, would prove as hurtfull for the one, as helpfull for the other. Yea, not onely will a skilful! and wary physician be carefull to use no cure but that which is fit for that sort of disease, but he will also consider all other circumstances, and make the remedies sutable therunto; as the temperature of the clime where the patient is, the constitution of the planets, the time of the moone, the season of the yeere, the age and complexion of the patient, and the present state of his body, in strength or weaknes. For one cure must not ever be used for the selfesame disease, but according to the varying of any of the foresaid circumstances, that sort of remedy must be used which is fittest for the same. Where by the contrary in this case, such is the miraculous omnipotencie of our strong tasted tobacco, as it cures al sorts of diseases (which never any drugge could do before) in all persons, and at all times. It cures all maner of distillations, either in the head or stomacke (if you beleeve their axiomes) although in very deed it doe both corrupt the braine, and by causing over quicke digestion, fill the stomacke full of crudities. It cures the gout in the feet, and (which is miraculous) in that very instant when the smoke thereof, as light, flies up into the head, the vertue therof, as heavy, runs down to the litle toe. It helps all sorts of agues. It makes a man sober that was drunk. It refreshes a weary man and yet makes a man hungry. Being taken when they goe to bed, it makes one sleepe soundly, and yet being taken when a man is sleepie and drowsie, it will, as they say, awake his braine and quicken his understanding. As for curing of the pockes, it serves for that use but among the pockie Indian slaves. Here in England it is refined, and will not deigne to cure here any other then cleanly and gentlemanly diseases. O omnipotent power of tobacco! And if it could by the smoake thereof chase out devils, as the smoake of Tobias fish did (which I am sure could smell no stronglier), it would serve for a precious relicke, both for the superstitious priests, and the insolent puritanes to cast out devils withall.

Admitting then, and not confessing, that the use thereof were healthful for some sorts of diseases, should it be used for all sicknesses? Should it be used by all men? Should it be used at all times? Yea, should it be used by able, yong, strong, healthful men? Medicine hath that vertue, that it never leaves a man in that state wherein it finds him. It makes a sicke man whole, but a whole man sicke. And as medicine helps nature, being taken at times of necessitie, so being ever and continually used, it doeth but weaken, weary and weare nature. What speake I of medicine? Nay, let a man every houre of the day, or as oft as many in this countrey use to take tobacco, let a man, I say, but take as oft the best sorts of nourishments in meate and drinke that can be devised, he shall with the continuall use thereof weaken both his head and his stomacke. All his members shall become feeble, his spirits dull, and in the end, as a drowsie lazie belly-god, he shall evanish in a lethargic.

And from this weaknesse it proceeds, that many in this kingdome have had such a continuall use of taking this unsavorie smoake, as now they are not able to forbeare the same, no more then an old drunkard can abide to be long sober, without falling into an incurable weaknesse and evill constitution, for their continuall custome hath made to them, *habitum, alteram, naturam*, so to those that from their birth have bene continually nourished upon poison and things venemous, wholsome meats are only poisonable.

Thus having, as I trust, sufficiently answered the most principall arguments that are used in defence of this vile custome, it rests only to informe you what sinnes and vanities you commit in the filthie abuse thereof. First, are you not guiltie of sinnefull and shamefull lust (for lust may be as well in any of the senses as in feeling) that although you be troubled with no disease, but in perfect health, yet can you neither be merry at an ordinary, nor lascivious in the stewes, if you lacke tobacco to provoke your appetite to any of those sorts of recreation, lusting after it as the children of Israel did in the wildernesse after quailes? Secondly it is, as you use or rather abuse it, a branch of the sinne of drunkennes, which is the root of all sinnes. For as the only delight that drunkards take in wine is the strength of the taste and the force of the fume therof, that mounts up to the braine (for no drunkards love any weake, or sweete drinke) so are not those (I meane the strong heate and the fume) the onely qualities that make tobacco so delectable to all the lovers of it? And as no man likes strong heady drinke the first day (because *nemo repente fit turpissimus*) but by custome is piece and piece allured, while in the ende, a drunkard will have as great a thirst to be drunke, as a sober man to quench his thirst with a draught when hee hath need of it, so is not this the very case of all the great takers of tobacco, which therefore they themselves do attribute to a bewitching qualitie in it? Thirdly, is it not the greatest sinne of all, that you the people of all sorts of this kingdome, who are created and ordeined by God, to bestow both your persons and goods, for the maintenance both of the honour and safety of your King and Commonwealth, should disable your selves in both? In your persons having by this continuall vile custome brought your selves to this shamefull imbecilitie, that you are not able to ride or walke the journey of a Jewes sabboth, but you must have a reekie cole brought you from the next poore house to kindle your tobacco with? Whereas he cannot be thought able for any service in the warres, that cannot endure oftentimes the want of meat, drinke and sleepe, much more then must he endure the want of tobacco. In the times of the many glorious and victorious battailes fought by this nation, there was no word of tobacco. But now if it were time of warres, and that you were to make some sudden cavalcado upon your enemies, if any of you should seeke leisure to stay behinde his fellow for taking of tobacco, for my part I should never be sorry for any evill chance that might befall him. To take a custome in any thing that cannot be left againe, is most harmful to the people of any land. Mollicies and delicacie were the wracke and overthrow, first of the Persian, and next of the Romane empire. And this very custome of taking tobacco (whereof our present purpose is) is even at this day accounted so effeminate among the Indians themselves, as in the market they will offer no price for a slave to be sold, whom they find to be a great tobacco taker.

Now how you are by this custome disabled in your goods, let the gentry of this land beare witnesse, some of them bestowing three, some foure hundred pounds a yeere upon this precious stinke, which I am sure might be bestowed upon many farre better uses. I read indeed of a knavish courtier, who for abusing the favour of the Emperour Alexander Severus his master, by taking bribes to intercede for sundry persons in his masters eare (for whom he never once opened his mouth), was justly choked with smoke, with this doome, *fumo pereat, qui fumum vendidit*. But of so many smoke-buyers, as are at this present in this kingdome, I never read nor heard.

And for the vanities committed in this filthy custome, is it not both great vanitie and uncleannesse, that at the table, a place of respect, of cleanlinesse, of modestie, men should not be ashamed, to sit tossing of tobacco pipes and puffing of the smoke of tobacco one to another, making the filthy smoke and stinke thereof, to exhale athwart the dishes and infect the aire, when very often, men that abhorre it are at their repast? Surely smoke becomes a kitchin farre better then a dining chamber and yet it makes a kitchin also oftentimes in the inward parts of men, soyling and infecting them, with an unctuous and oily kind of soote, as hath bene found in some great tobacco takers, that after their death were opened. And not onely meate time, but no other time nor action is exempted from the publike use of this uncivill tricke, so as if the wives of Diepe list to contest with this nation for good maners, their worst maners would in all reason be found at least not so dishonest (as ours are) in this point. The publike use whereof, at all times, and in all places, hath now so farre prevailed, as divers men very sound both in judgement and complexion, have bene at last forced to take it also without desire, partly because they were ashamed to seeme singular (like the two philosophers that were forced to ducke themselves in that raine water, and so become fooles as well as the rest of the people) and partly, to be as one that was content to eate garlicke (which he did not love) that he might not be troubled with the smell of it in the breath of his fellowes. And is it not a great vanitie, that a man cannot heartily welcome his friend now, but straight they must be in hand with tobacco? No it is become in place of a cure, a point of good fellowship, and hee that will refuse to take a pipe of tobacco among his fellowes (though by his owne election hee would rather feele the favour of a sinke) is accounted peevish and no good company, even as they doe with tipling in the colde easterne countreys. Yea, the mistresse cannot in a more manerly kind, entertaine her senant, then by giving him out of her faire hand a pipe of tobacco. But herein is not only a great vanity, but a great contempt of Gods good giftes, that the sweetnesse of mans breath, being a good gift of God, should be wilfully corrupted by this stinking smoke, wherin I must confesse, it hath too strong a vertue. And so, that which is an ornament of nature, and can neither by any artifice be at the first acquired, nor once lost, be recovered againe, shalbe filthily corrupted with an incurable stinke, which vile qualitie is as directly contrary to that wrong opinion which is holden of the wholesomnesse therof, as the venime of putrifaction is contrary to the vertue preservative.

Moreover, which is a great iniquitie, and against all humanitie, the husband shall not be ashamed, to reduce therby his delicate, wholesom and cleane complexioned wife, to that extremity, that either she must also corrupt her sweet breath therwith, or els resolve to live in a perpetual stinking torment.

Have you not reason then to be ashamed and to forbeare this filthy noveltie, so basely grounded, so foolishly received, and so grossely mistaken in the right use thereof; in your abuse thereof sinning against God, harming your selves both in persons and goods, and raking also thereby the markes and notes of vanitie upon you; by the custome thereof making your selves to be wondered at by all forreine civill nations, and by all strangers that come among you, to be scorned and contemned? A custome loathsome to the eye, hatefull to the nose, harmefull to the braine, dangerous to the lungs, and in the blacke stinking fume thereof, neerest resembling the horrible Stigian smoake of the pit that is bottomlesse.

James VI

RENAISSANCE SONNETS

'In Orkney'

Vpon the vtmost corners of the warld,
and on the borders of this massiue round,
quhaire fates and fortoune hither hes me harld,
I doe deplore my greiffs vpon this ground;
and seing roring seis from roks rebound
by ebbs and streames of contrair routing tyds,
and phebus chariot in there wawes ly dround,
quha equallye now night and day devyds,
I call to mynde the storms my thoughts abyds,
which euer wax and never dois decrees,
for nights of dole dayes Ioys ay euer hyds,
and in there vayle doith al my weill suppress:
  so this I see, quhaire euer I remove,
   I chainge bot sees, but can not chainge my love.

William Fowler (1560–1612)

'First Jove, as greatest God above the rest'

First *Ioue*, as greatest God aboue the rest,
Graunt thou to me a pairt of my desyre:
That when in verse of thee I wryte my best,
This onely thing I earnestly requyre,

That thou my veine Poetique so inspyre,
As they may suirlie think, all that it reid,
When I descryue thy might and thundring fyre,
That they do see thy self in verie deid
From heauen thy greatest *Thunders* for to leid,
And syne vpon the *Gyants* heads to fall:
Or cumming to thy *Semele* with speid
In *Thunders* least, at her request and call:
   Or throwing *Phaethon* downe from heauen to eard,
   With threatning thunders, making monstrous reard.

James VI (1566–1625)

'To his Mistress'

So suete a kis yistrene[1] fra thee I reft,
   In bouing doun thy body on the bed,
   That evin my Iyfe within thy lippis I left;
Sensyne[2] from thee my spirits wald neuer shed;
To folou thee it from my body fled,
   And left my corps als cold as ony kie.[3]
   Bot vhen the danger of my death I dred,
   To seik my spreit I sent my harte to thee;
Bot it wes so inamored with thyn ee,
   With thee it myndit lykuyse[4] to remane:
   So thou hes keepit captive all the thrie,
   More glaid to byde then to returne agane.
Except thy breath thare places had suppleit,
Euen in thyn armes thair doutles had I deit.

Alexander Montgomerie (*c.*1545–*c.*1610)

1. *yesternight*
2. *since then*
3. *key*
4. *likewise*

From 'The Tarantula of Love'

O cruell love, why dothe thow sore assayle
my humbled harte with torments overtorne?
quhat triumphs cost thow mereit of avayle
in thralling me who is so far forlorne?
and to quhat end is shee as yet forborne
who, cairles of thy flams, thy bowe and darte,
in her great pryde doeth all thy pouer scorne,

and dois remark my flams with frosen harte?
now through my loss I am maid more expert,
and now dois see to be bot taels and dremes
that thow hes Mars and that I ove him self subvert,
with phebus bright in his resplendent beames,
   sen that my dame, the glorye of myne eyes,
   dispyseth the, and dois disdayne my cryes.

                          William Fowler (1560–1612)

'The tender snow, of granis soft and quhyt'

The tender snow, of granis soft & quhyt,
   Is nocht so sone conswmit vith phebus heit,
As is my breist, beholding my delyte,
   Pyneit[1] vith the presence of my lady sueit.
The surging seyis, with stormie streameis repleit,
   Tormoylit nocht the wandring shipis sa sair.
As absence dois torment my werie spreit,
   Fleitting a flocht[2] betuixt hoip & dispair.
My cative corps consumis with cursed cair;
   Mistrust & dreid hes baneist[3] esperance,
That I am forceit to perische quhae sould mair,
   & trast the wyte[4] upon rememberance;
Than absence, presence, remembrance, all thre,
Torment me for hir saik eternallie.

                   Alexander Montgomerie (*c*.1545-*c*.1610)

1. *pained*
2. *afloat*
3. *banished*
4. *blame*

INDEX OF EXEMPLARS

EXEMPLAR SEQUENCE IN VOLUME

EXEMPLARS BY STAGES OF THE SCHOOL

S1/2

S3/4

S5/6

NOTES ON CONTRIBUTORS

James N. Alison is former Staff HMI for English and Secretary of the Association for Scottish Literary Studies.

Anne Donovan is Assistant Principal Teacher of English at Hillhead High School in Glasgow.

David Drever is Principal Teacher of English at Kirkwall Grammar School in Orkney.

Morna Fleming is Principal Teacher of English at Beath High School in Cowdenbeath, Fife.

Gordon Gibson is Co-ordinator of Language Studies in the Faculty of Education, University of Paisley.

Anne Gifford is Lecturer in Language Studies in the Faculty of Education at the University of Paisley.

Dr Douglas Gifford is Professor of Scottish Literature at the University of Glasgow.

John Hodgart is Principal Teacher of English at Garnock Academy in Kilbirnie, Ayrshire.

Alan MacGillivray is former Senior Lecturer in English at Jordanhill College in Glasgow and Honorary Lecturer at the University of Strathclyde.

Dr James McGonigal is Head of Language and Literature at St Andrew's College in Bearsden, Glasgow.

Neil McMillan is in the Department of Scottish Literature at the University of Glasgow.

Ronald Renton is Deputy Rector of St Aloysius' College in Glasgow and Convenor of the Schools/FE Committee for the Association for Scottish Literary Studies.

George Sutherland is Examinations Officer (English) for the Scottish Qualifications Authority.